Free

Embrace Your Transformation!

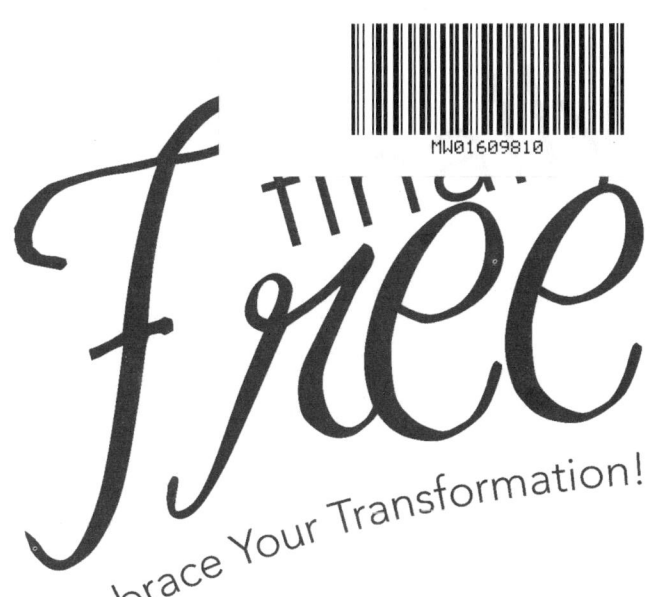

SYLVIA FERRIN

FINALLY FREE
Embrace Your Transformation!

Second Printing, 2020

ISBN 978-0-9800943-3-6

All Scripture references are from the KJV of the Bible.

Cover design by Chase Stamp

Author Photograph by Bill Ferrin at the Butterfly Palace, Branson, Missouri

NOTE TO BUTTERFLY LOVERS: The more accurate name for the casing around a growing butterfly is chrysalis, rather than cocoon. Cocoon is the term usually applied to moths and other insects that undergo a similar transformation as butterflies. For the purposes of this book, however, statements like "a butterfly emerging from its cocoon" flow better than "a butterfly emerging from its chrysalis." The author offers her apologies for taking license with the similar terms and trusts that readers will overlook this intentional discrepancy.

To order additional copies:
Website – www.magnifytheword.com
Online Bookstore – www.mkt.com/FerrinBookstore
Email – sylviaferrin@hotmail.com

Printed in the United States of America
by Litho Printers and Bindery
Cassville, Missouri 65625

CONTENTS

CHAPTER 1

Choosing Change

TRANSFORMATION

Most people are familiar with the life cycle of a butterfly. The transformation process from the beginning of the butterfly's life to its free flight is awe-inspiring.

What happens if a butterfly is unable to break out of its cocoon?

It dies.

God wants you to fly freely. He wants you to experience complete and total liberty. He does not want you to get partway through your transformation process, just to give up somewhere along the way.

Flying freely like a beautiful butterfly requires that we grow. Growth requires change. That is why the first chapter of this book is called "Choosing Change." Before we can progress, we must choose to change, with the help of God.

Change is not easy for anyone, myself included. Yet, change is necessary for everyone who desires abundant life in Christ.

As God tries to change things in your life, don't dig in your heels. Change is difficult, yes, but to God it is beautiful.

There is something beautiful about a butterfly in its cocoon. You can see the vibrant colors and the marvelous life about to escape from its cocoon. The butterfly, seen through the translucent layer of the cocoon, is a promise of a release on its way.

What the transformation process means is that we are becoming more like Jesus and that we are shedding from our lives things that we no longer need. In God's eyes, this transformation process is beautiful!

VOLCANIC ERUPTION

When I was eight years old, Mount St. Helens erupted in fiery fury.

Not long after, I read a book about the disaster. It told the story of Harry Randall Truman, an elderly man who lived alone in a mountain cabin at the foot of the mountain. As the volcano began to rumble inside the earth – a precursor of the death and destruction to come – people were ordered to evacuate their homes.

But this one old man refused to leave. To those who pleaded with him to move to a safer place he said, "If the mountain goes, I'm going with it." He had lived near the mountain for over 50 years. It was his home.

The volcano exploded and tons of mud, uprooted trees, and dislodged boulders surged down the mountain, destroying everything in its path…including the old man.

We will never know why this man valued his familiar surroundings more than his very life. His voice is silent. He cannot tell us what motivated him to choose death over change.

All we know is that the mountain was his home. He was comfortable there and attached to it.

Because Harry Randall Truman chose comfort, he lost. Relocation was not an option for him because his attachment to his way of life – no matter how temporary and fragile – was his priority. Preserving the familiar was more important to him than preserving his life.

FIGHTING CHANGE

Many of us view our lives the same way. Sure, we would evacuate our houses if physical danger threatened our lives, if a flood or volcano were inevitable.

But how many times do we refuse to change our behavior or deeply entrenched mindsets because we prefer comfort to safety and we value familiarity more than peace?

People will fight change, even if it means it will revolutionize their lives for the better. I have met people who would prefer to live depressed and tormented rather than do things God's way and experience constant peace and joy.

Why? Because as strange as it sounds, living with depression, fear, anxiety, and worry is all they know. They don't want to leave their comfort zone.

SUBTLE CAPTORS

We tend to think of things like alcoholism and drug addiction as really big sins and we encourage people to seek God for deliverance from them.

But there are much more subtle captors that try to imprison us: Stress, an obsessive desire to achieve, love of money and possessions, worry, anxiety, fear, negativity, cynicism, unbalanced emotions, and gossip.

We like to overlook and minimize the effect of these and other seemingly harmless captors in our minds and lives. Strangely, because they are so much a part of our lives, we are comfortable with them.

Yet, these not-so-obvious enemies are just as potentially deadly and self-defeating as alcoholism and drug addiction. They can steal our peace, destroy family relationships, thwart God's purpose for our lives, and deflate our passion for the things of God.

You don't have to live that way. You don't have to live a defeated life. It is not necessary, nor is it God's will.

You don't have to put up with the lies and tactics of the enemy. Christ has made you free. He has unlocked the doors of your prison. If you are still in prison – bound by fear, negativity, or unhealthy emotions – only your mindset is keeping you there.

Don't continue to huddle in your prison cell. You don't have to keep looking out to freedom, longing for the day when abundant life will be a reality for you. You have a choice!

CHOOSING CHANGE

Some things do not change until *we* change. For example, people who want to lose 50 pounds but don't want to change their poor eating habits will probably not lose weight. They want the weight to disappear but they do not want to do anything to help the weight loss process.

Things don't change on their own. Stress, anxiety, and addiction to busyness do not go away on their own. Our relationships with the ones we love will not improve unless we make changes to the way we think, the way we talk, and our behavior.

Some things simply do not change until it becomes *our will* for them to change.

A person must *want* to change. I have met many people who had all the resources they needed to help them change: A wise pastor, believers to pray for them and support them, the Word of God to help them defeat every enemy. Yet, they were unwilling to make the changes necessary to enjoy complete liberty.

THINGS PEOPLE SAY

There are things people say that are nothing more than excuses for not altering their behavior. If you have found yourself thinking or saying any of these things, make a choice today to abandon your excuses. Trade them in for a superior life of complete liberty in Christ!

- "*I'm too old to change.*" What you really mean: My age should exempt me from changing.
- "*If everyone else changes, then I will change.*" What you really mean: Everyone else needs to change more than I do.
- "*This is just the way I was raised.*" What you really mean: I don't want to change.
- "*I'm waiting for God to change me.*" What you really mean: I don't fully understand that spiritual growth, good relationships, and emotional health are not all God's responsibility. There are things I need to do also.
- "*I can't think of anything in my life that needs to change.*" What you really mean: I don't want to admit my own faults.
- "*It's too much work to change.*" What you really mean: I like myself just fine the way I am.
- "*I can't change.*" What you really mean: I am too stubborn to change.

If you said "Ouch!" to any of these excuses and resent your excuses being exposed for what they are, don't worry. You are in the same boat with the rest of humanity. When confronted with the need to change, nearly all of us respond with pride, not humility.

ABANDONING EXCUSES

Often, we know what we should be doing. In fact, you will probably already know and will agree with a lot of this book's content.

But the painful question is: Are you actually attempting to draw closer to God by removing the obstacles in your life that are like roadblocks between you and Jesus?

Knowledge without application is like a car without wheels. It is not going anywhere. It is useless. We must take what we know and apply it to our lives.

Let's determine that – with the help of the Lord – we are going to stop relying on our flimsy, worn out excuses and progress in our walk with God. Trade in those excuses for a vibrant relationship with the One who loves you more than anyone else!

CONSCIOUS CHANGE

Change is easier for some people than for others, but it is not super-easy for anyone. Consider this: You have been taking the same route to work for 10 years. Then, someone tells you about another route that you never knew about. It will reduce your commute by 15 minutes. You decide to start going that way.

But you are accustomed to traveling down the same roads you been using for years. You forget to take the new route. You have formed a pattern in your life. It takes *conscious effort* to remind yourself to take the better route. Even after you make the initial change, you might subconsciously slip back into your old pattern.

Change requires consistent focus on replacing an old habit with a new one.

Although Christ liberates us from the power of sin and death, letting go of unbiblical concepts is our choice. Freedom from these concepts will not just fall into our laps. If we want to be free, we must choose change. Just as a butterfly works its way out of its comfortable and cozy cocoon, we must put forth a deliberate, conscious effort to break free from the mindsets that keep us bound.

CONTINUAL CHANGE

I have observed that when people begin following Jesus, they make a lot of dramatic changes to their lifestyles during the early stages of their walk with Him. As a result, their lives greatly improve.

But at some point, many Christians become comfortable with their lives. They do not continue to grow. They no longer extract the little, seemingly insignificant, weeds from their lives but allow certain remnants of the "old man" to linger in their lives. So they stagnate.

But as Christians, we are under a mandate to progress, to go forward, to leave behind unbelief, self-will, self-reliance, and certain patterns of living that are displeasing to God.

You may have been living for God for a long time. You might not need to completely change your life because you have already applied the Word to your life in many different areas. Yet, perhaps you know that you are not living in complete spiritual liberty. It could be that just one or two roadblocks are in your way.

The Christian life is one of continual change. We cannot afford to stop growing, to stop changing, to stop becoming more like Jesus. Yes, we can enjoy our relationship with God and be thankful for the closeness we have with Him.

But He has an unlimited supply of blessings! Why not access them by removing obstacles – even small ones – that hinder our relationship with Him? God will have as deep of a relationship with us as we will allow.

AUTHENTIC CHANGE

Why doesn't God make us "perfect" the day we are born again? Why doesn't He take away all our issues and hang-ups in one fell swoop? Why doesn't He instantly remove all of our anxiety, intimidation and insecurities with a snap of His fingers?

God is more interested in developing our character than He is in our comfort. By gently nudging us away from our comfort zone, He is inviting us to trust Him with things that we have never trusted Him before. He wants us to grow, to mature, and to become more like Him.

Some people want God to give them a "magic pill" of sorts and remove all their problems and hang-ups. But they don't want to make any changes to their lives. They want the benefits of change but they don't actually want to help the process.

God wants us to acknowledge our flaws and weaknesses. Then, He wants us to work on changing them. Change requires action. Work is necessary. The good thing is that we don't have to do this alone. He will be with us every step of the way. As we become more open and transparent with Him, we will find our relationship with Him deepening and growing stronger and more authentic.

ONE-ON-ONE MINISTRY

The good thing is that if you truly love the Lord and you want to become more Christ-like, God will enable you to change. He does expect cooperation on your part, but He will empower you to make changes that you can't make on your own. As you pray, read His Word, and diligently cultivate your relationship with Him, you will find it easier and easier to change things that once looked insurmountable.

As you read *Finally Free*, read slowly and deliberately. Don't let this be just another book that you whiz through and then lay aside. Allow God to speak to you about things in your own life that need to change. Instead of skimming over difficult issues in your heart and life, take them to the Lord in prayer.

As God begins to draw to your attention things that need to change, take time to stop and pray and seek the Lord. Allow Him to minister to you in times of prayer. It is those one-on-one times with God that will make all the difference in your life.

THANK GOD

The need to change does not mean that you are a horrible person. It simply means that you are human. When God speaks to you about something in your life that needs to change, rather than resent what you might consider His unwelcome intrusion into your life, be thankful that He loves you enough to draw you into a deeper relationship with Him.

Thank God for all He has done in your life to this point. Thank Him for deliverances He has wrought for you and all the good things He has put into your life.

Then, thank Him for helping you to admit that there are still things that need to change. Thank Him for helping you shed your excuses and continue to be transformed into His likeness.

Thank God for the deeper relationship with Him that He has in store as you continue to acknowledge the areas of your life that need to change. Thank Him for not giving up on you but continuing to draw you to Him!

SPIRITUAL METAMORPHOSIS

The New Testament contains a theme of change, of continual progression. II Peter 3:18 encourages us to "grow in grace, and in the knowledge of our Lord and Saviour Jesus Christ." This is a sample of many New Testament Scriptures which encourage us to not stop, slow down, or become comfortable, but to grow.

The apostle Paul said that he had not yet attained. He admitted that he was not yet perfect. He did not believe or act as though he had arrived at the peak of spiritual perfection. He still needed to continue to reach and "press toward the mark for the prize of the high calling of God in Christ Jesus" (Philippians 3:12-14).

We can use the apostle Paul's example as a guide for our own lives. The spiritual metamorphosis that takes place is a process. Romans 12:2 tells us to not be conformed to this world, but to be transformed by the renewing of our minds.

Here in Romans 12:2, the Greek word for "transformed" is "metamorphoo." This Greek word is where we get our word "metamorphosis" that describes how a slow-moving earthbound caterpillar morphs into a free-flying butterfly.

This marvelous and fascinating object lesson from nature illustrates how God wants to make something beautiful of our lives. As we submit our lives and minds to God's hands and allow Him to mold us, step-by-step a marvelous spiritual transformation takes place.

WORTH THE CHANGE

If you have reached this point in this first chapter, "Congratulations!" This is perhaps the most difficult-to-accept chapter in this book.

We sometimes pretend that we don't know what is keeping us from complete freedom in Christ. But I think that, although our pride keeps us from admitting them, we all know our weaknesses

It is always difficult to honestly admit that we need to change, but when we realize that changing to become more like Jesus is a good thing, not a bad thing, we have won half of our battles. *Once we change our mindset about change, the actual changes become much easier.*

Sure, change can be difficult. Change is rarely comfortable. It requires that we break free of long held beliefs.

As we take steps in the right direction, we find that the prize at the end is worth the effort. The world we enter is superior to the one we leave behind. The rewards far outnumber the sacrifices.

LIBERATED AT LAST

By changing your mindsets and habits that do not agree with life in Christ, you will find yourself truly transformed by the power of the Word and Spirit of God. You will be able to say, "I am liberated at last! I am finally free."

A butterfly must struggle to escape its cocoon. It must become dissatisfied with its cozy environment and want freedom more than comfort.

The amazing thing is that without the struggle, the butterfly dies. The butterfly beats its wings against the inside of the cocoon as it tries to escape. This process strengthens the wings. The fight is what ultimately gives the butterfly the power to fly. If a person sees the butterfly struggling inside the cocoon and breaks open the cocoon prematurely, the butterfly will not have enough strength to fly and it will die.

Don't be afraid to fight your way out of your comfort zone. The process might be painful and you might be tempted to stop fighting. But the very process of breaking out that seems so difficult is the same process that will give you the ability to freely fly and soar high.

If you will just take one step away from your comfort zone – the very place that will destroy you if you stay – then you will find yourself in a place of liberty you've never known before. You will love your new life.

It will definitely be worth the change.

CHAPTER 2

Stress Solutions

WARNING: STRESS AHEAD

After my husband read "A Day of Stress" (the following section in this chapter), I asked him what he thought of it.

He said, "It is kind of overwhelming."

"Good," I said. "That is exactly the feeling I want to convey. For some women, the stress level I portray in this fictional story is an every day reality. They will be able to identify with it completely."

Of course, not everyone's life is quite this stressful. Some people discover effective methods for managing stress and do not allow themselves to become overwhelmed, no matter how challenging life gets.

But for those of you who wonder if life has a "pause" button, this chapter is for you. There are answers. There is hope.

A DAY OF STRESS

You wake at 5:30 a.m. After a few quiet moments, the rest of the family begins to stir and the house becomes alive with motion and noise. You prepare a simple breakfast and get the kids ready for school. After you take them to school, you came back home, wash dishes, throw a load of laundry in the washing machine, and quickly pay a few bills.

Then, you help your husband pack for his out-of-town business trip. As the two of you hurriedly get his belongings together, he rattles off a list of things he needs you to do while he is gone. He leaves in a rush and you leave soon after for work.

For the hundredth time, you wish that you didn't have to work outside the home but you live in a metropolitan area and the price of even a small house is astronomical. Your closest friends have big homes and nice cars and you want the same, even though it makes life a little more stressful than you would like. You justify the extra expense by saying that you want your children to have the best you can give them.

Your commute to work is hectic. People are driving as though they are practicing for the Indy 500. You arrive at work already mentally fatigued from the strain of the busy morning.

You walk into the office and a co-worker passes you a pile of papers. She has to leave early today. Can you handle part of her workload? "Sure," you say.

About 10 a.m., you are struggling with the new computer program the company insists is better than the last. But it has so many glitches it hardly seems worthwhile. Today, trying to figure it out backs up your progress significantly.

You skip your lunch break because you have so much to do.

At 2:00 p.m. your boss walks by and tosses an order on your desk. "This is priority. It needs to be done today before you go," he says.

You look at it in despair. It is a major project! Your desk already looks like a tornado had been by. *He wants this done today*?

You are tired and hungry and it shows in your attitude. You sigh in exasperation and resign yourself to a late day at work. You call a friend to pick your kids up from school.

Suddenly you remember that you are scheduled to work at church tonight. There is an important fundraiser supper and you've been asked to be on the cleanup crew. Great. You dig into your work and barely get it done two hours past the time you normally leave. You speed home, hoping that all the state troopers are elsewhere.

When you get home, your kids immediately ask, "Where have you been? We're starving!"

Wrong thing to say! You toss your purse and computer case on the sofa and head for the kitchen.

As you open the refrigerator, the phone rings. A telemarketer. You interrupt his spiel by rudely hanging up on him.

You turn back to the fridge, then realize that the ingredients you need are at the store. Forget it. You call the local pizza joint.

When the pizza arrives, there are mushrooms on it, which the kids hate. They grumble. You snap at them and tell them to pick off the mushrooms and quit complaining.

They ask you if you drank pickle juice on the way home. Obviously, they are not going to think you are the coolest person on the planet tonight.

Your stepson is especially irritable. You sense his rebellious attitude toward you. He came to live with you a few months earlier. He is 13, a tough age for any kid, but he's resentful of you as his replacement mother. Whenever your husband – his father – is gone on business trips, his resentment and anger skyrocket.

You think to yourself, *This is going to be one long week*.

During your not-so-gourmet dinner, the phone rings again. It's the church fundraiser coordinator.

"Can you get to the church as soon as possible? Jan, who was going to serve food, isn't feeling good and can't help tonight. We need you to fill in for her."

Never one to say, "No," you throw away your dinnerware – paper plates – and clear the table.

When you get to church, the kitchen is a zoo. Everyone is rushing around trying to get things done.

While you are trying to figure out what to do, your younger sister calls on your cell phone. She and her husband have not been getting along and she wants to talk it out. You think, *I don't have time for this*! Plus, you have enough problems of your own. But you listen anyway, as the other workers peek around the corner at you, wondering why you are yakking on the phone when you are supposed to be working.

Finally, at 12:45 a.m., you grab a towel and dry your hands. As you turn from the church's kitchen sink, your hand grasps your aching back as you stand up straight too quickly. You have been bending over the sink for hours, washing what seemed like an endless stream of dirty dishes.

You are exhausted. You say a quick goodbye to the few people still at the church and head for your car.

As you drive home on the nearly deserted streets, you wonder, *Does life ever slow down*?

A CASE OF NERVES

Although stress levels vary, we all have external stressors that tend to drain us of our joy and make us frazzled and irritable.

When I was a kid, nobody used the word "stress." I'm not sure when it came into common use, but I think the term people used instead of "stress" was "nerves."

"She has a bad case of nerves," you would hear people say.

To my kid-mind, "a case of nerves" sounded medical, serious, and a little mysterious.

Now we say, “I’m so stressed” or “I’m stressed out.” And it seems like most everyone talks about how much stress they have. If we were living in the old days, there would sure be a lot of people with “a bad case of nerves.”

POWERLESS?

Can we do anything about stress? Is it a problem without a remedy? Because our lives are fast-paced and filled with pressure on all sides, is stress something we have to resign ourselves to living with?

Is stress a badge of honor we wear to let everyone know we are high achievers? Do we think that since we do so much and have so much responsibility that stress is the obligatory price we must pay for our hard work?

Is stress more powerful than we are?

EMPOWERED

We can become so used to stress that we think it is normal to live with it in our lives, day in and day out.

But we are not powerless to control our stress level. We do not have to allow stress to rule our lives. With all of the promises God makes available to us, we have at our disposal the opportunity to live with a lot less stress than we put up with.

Yes, life will bring stressful situations our way. But we do not have to be overwhelmed by them. Our lives will never be free from adversity. But our lives can be free from that anxious, troubled, stressed-out, tense, overwhelmed feeling.

External stress does not mean that we have to allow internal stress to have power over our lives. We can't control everything about our lives but we can control how we respond.

In the kingdom of God, stress can be a bit overrated. By believing and activating the Word of God, we can prevent the overwhelming stress that causes mental disorders and nervous breakdowns. God has empowered us with the ability to control the effect stress has on our lives.

STRESS SOLUTION

God is not unsympathetic toward us regarding the stress in our lives. In fact, He is very compassionate and understanding.

But He offers more than compassion and understanding. He offers a solution. He tells us how we can de-stress our lives.

The word "stress" is not used in the Bible. But words like "overwhelmed," "careful," and "troubled" mean about the same thing as "stressed."

God's stress solution is so simple that most people won't accept it. They want some difficult-to-understand answer that takes, well, a lot of stress to figure out! We will discuss self-imposed stress and offer some stress reduction tips, but here is the core solution:

"When my heart is overwhelmed: lead me to the rock that is higher than I" (Psalm 61:2).

There it is in a nutshell. When stress threatens to take you down, look up to the One with limitless strength. When you think you will melt under the pressures of life, go to the Rock that can never be moved.

God's shoulders are big enough to carry you and all your problems. Quit trying to figure everything out on your own. God did not design you with the ability to carry such heavy loads; that is His job. When you are burdened down by life, talk to Him.

Trust God. Rest in Him. Cast your cares on Him. That is His plan. And it works. It is the best stress solution.

SELF-IMPOSED STRESS

I Corinthians 10:13 is an oft-quoted verse: "There hath no temptation taken you but such as is common to man: but God is faithful, who will not suffer you to be tempted above that ye are able; but will with the temptation also make a way to escape, that ye may be able to bear it."

The word "temptation" can refer not just to the lure of sin, but also to adversity and problems. Sounds a bit like "stress." In this verse, God promises that He will not allow more adversity in our lives than we are able to bear. What an amazing, loving, kind God!

But guess what? God is kinder to us than we are to ourselves because *we* sometimes put more upon ourselves than we can bear! While God is trying to lighten our load, we work really hard to attach big boulders to our backs. He tries to make our walk easier, and we try to make it harder.

This is called self-imposed stress. It is what we do when we buy a car that we know we can't afford. It is what we do when we try to change people instead of praying for them, stepping out of the way, and allowing God to work in their lives. It is what we do when we allow our priorities to get out of whack. We invite stress into our lives that is completely unnecessary. God did not put it there; we did.

We should look with suspicion at anyone or anything that threatens to steal our peace. For example, if that car is too expensive for your budget, don't buy it, no matter how much you like it. Buy something more affordable.

Don't impose stress upon your own life that is completely avoidable. Enough trials will come your way without creating some of your own.

Think long-term. How will this choice affect my life? Will it create peace or confusion?

Don't be a glutton for punishment. Don't stress yourself out!

STRESS REDUCTION TIPS

Here are some practical tips for reducing stress in your life.

The goal of these stress reduction tips is not to eliminate all of our responsibilities so we can sit on the sofa all day eating bon-bons. The answer to reducing stress is not withdrawing from life, people, and responsibilities.

Rather, our goal is to be as productive as possible without being overwhelmed by stress and anxiety. When we learn how to rely on God despite external stressors, when we make proper choices, and when we eliminate self-imposed stress, we will actually become *more* productive.

- *Put God first in your life.*

Keep God Number One in your life, heart and mind. Don't allow anyone or anything to displace Him from the center of your heart. This alone will eliminate much of your stress because putting God first gives us peace.

- *Pray.*

This is elementary but we all need to be reminded that prayer is the best stress reliever. It will eliminate your anxiety. It will calm you even when you have much to do.

Prayer is something we know to do but often do not do. Even if you are extremely busy, take at least a few minutes to pray, to read at least a verse of Scripture, and to meditate on the Word.

This might not seem like much, and you know you need more prayer time, but just because you don't have hours to pray does not mean you should neglect prayer completely.

- *Identify your biggest stressors.*

Marriage problems? Seek help from your pastor and focus on improving your marriage.

Financial difficulties? Do all you can to reduce your debt and get help with managing your finances.

Sick? Not always, of course, but often our sickness is the result of our own poor choices. Don't accept your sickness as irreversible. Trust in God for healing and change the behavior that made you sick in the first place.

These are just three examples of common stressors. Identify *your* biggest stressors and then work to ease their strain on your life.

- *Live within your means.*

If you overextend yourself financially, you are creating your own stress. If your car payment is more than you can afford, sell your car and get a cheaper one. If you like expensive clothes, shop less often and realize that your worth does not come from what you wear. If you can't afford a big house with a big house payment and costly utility bills, downsize.

Poor financial choices are one of the biggest causes of self-imposed stress.

- *Prioritize your life.*

Most people are not good at juggling. Sooner or later they will drop a ball and if they get too overwhelmed, the whole routine will come crashing down around them.

What is most important in your life? Make a list and focus on what is at the top of the list.

- *Say "No."*

For high achievers, this is hard to do. But if you want to reduce your stress level, realize that you just can't do all things well. It is okay to occasionally say "No."

God knows that you are willing to work but He also knows that you are a human being with limitations.

- *Ask for help.*

Don't try to do everything yourself. Asking for help does not mean that you are shirking your job. It means that you recognize that one person can only do so much.

- *Quit trying to be Miss/Mrs./Mr. Perfect.*

You cannot excel at everything. Quit bemoaning what you don't do well and spend time honing your natural, God-given talents.

- *Simplify your life.*

What unnecessary things can you cut out of your life? Simplifying your life will help you focus on the things that matter most.

- *Develop organizational skills.*

Make lists of the things you need to do so you do not get overwhelmed. Work smarter, not necessarily harder. Pre-planning can prevent frustration and increase your effectiveness.

- *Slow down.*

There is nothing beautiful about a rat race. Things will get done. Life is not going to slow down. You must slow yourself down.

- *Don't sweat the small stuff.*

And a lot of stuff is small stuff. Don't major on the minors.

- *Come to grips with the fact that you are not Superman/Superwoman.*

You cannot be everyone's hero. You cannot help everyone.

You cannot make people's choices for them. Do what you can, when you can, but leave the big stuff to God and allow others to make their own decisions.

Let Jesus be their hero.

- *Don't assume someone else's stress.*

Just because a family member, co-worker or friend has "a bad case of nerves" does not mean that you have to catch it from them. Keep your mind on God and His promises. You do not have to allow someone else's stress to infect you.

- *Don't react to situations from your emotions.*

Reacting emotionally creates undue stress. Before reacting, pray. Allow God to settle your spirit and give you direction.

Hear my cry, O God;
attend unto my prayer.
From the end of the earth will I cry unto thee,
when my heart is overwhelmed:
lead me to the rock that is higher than I.
For thou hast been a shelter for me,
and a strong tower from the enemy.
I will abide in thy tabernacle for ever:
I will trust in the covert of thy wings.
Selah.

Psalm 61:1-4

CHAPTER 3

The Busyness Business

THE POINT OF BUSY

American society is fast-paced. Often, the busier we are, the more important and successful we tend to feel, even though we are stressed to the max. We feel compelled to stay in step with our culture that keeps us going ninety-to-nothing morning till night.

At the end of the day, in our weariness, we sometimes wonder, "What on earth was the point of it all?"

Some people talk about how busy they are, but what are they actually achieving?

Henry David Thoreau said, "It is not enough to be busy. So are the ants. The question is: What are we busy about?"

BLESSING OR CURSE?

The Bible pointedly speaks against idleness, using unappealing words like "slothful" and "sluggard" to define lazy people. In the Bible, laziness and idleness are always referred to with disparaging terminology.

For many Americans, however, it is not idleness but busyness that taxes them physically and emotionally.

In their book *Revealed*, Linda Clare and Kristen Ingram say it well: "In the pre-Industrial Revolution times, a woman was expected to take care of the cooking, cleaning, and child rearing. In addition, she kept the home fires burning, made soap, candles, and other household products, and tended the garden. She might sew the family's clothes and keep them mended and darned to extend their wear. She taught the children to read and was in charge of their spiritual upbringing as well. The only time this woman had to herself was perhaps a few minutes in prayer. She rarely lived past sixty.

"You say you're glad you didn't live then? Well, today's women have only traded a full day of backbreaking housework for a full day of brain breaking deadlines, traffic jams, and day-care woes. It's enough to make you sick.

"Intent on buzzing around like busy bees, we often neglect our physical and emotional health. The Proverbs 31 woman dangles in front of us like a carrot, luring us to try harder. Squeeze in another assignment, take on one more project, until one day we simply can't do anymore. We're physically sick or at best overwhelmed. Busyness has claimed another victim."[1]

STOP TRYING TO DO IT ALL

Our society encourages overachievement. What is overachievement? Overachievement is achievement obtained at the expense of personal peace, physical rest, and spiritual health.

Some people are afraid of failure so they drive themselves to succeed and excel. Perhaps their parents placed unrealistic high expectations on them so they are afraid of being reprimanded if they don't do well.

We can busy ourselves with going everywhere, doing everything, and trying to keep everybody happy. But because we overexert ourselves, we get stressed and anxious and, as a result, are not much good to anybody.

Vonda Skelton writes, "Thanks to technology, feminism, the media and our culture, we believe the lie that says we not only *can* do it all, but that we *have to*. And Satan is quite happy with this deception – because he knows that even if he can't make us bad, he can make us busy."[2]

I once heard someone say that we need to learn to separate the urgent [essential and necessary] from the important. Some things might seem urgent to us, but in reality they are important but not urgent.

Certain things that we think are extremely significant today will be meaningless to us ten years from now.

Of course, our top priority should be our relationship with God. God does not want to be just one component of our lives. He wants to be the One around which all else in our lives revolve. Maintaining our personal peace through prayer and devotional reading and study of the Bible should be high on our priority list.

What we do for God and even praying for others should never take a backseat to our own relationship with God. If we don't keep God first in our lives – no matter how much we *do* for Him – our relationship with Him will suffer.

Next on the list should be our families. Spending time together and taking time to communicate is vital. Don't let life's busyness rob you of precious time with the ones you love the most.

All of the other things we do – tasks and errands, personal projects, household chores, and things like house renovations – should be properly prioritized, with God at the top of the list. The point is that we can't do it all, so we must first do those things that are necessary and essential.

We think, "If I don't do it, it won't get done." While that may be true, it really doesn't matter if some things get done. I have watched women stress about decorating their homes for Christmas. They want everything to be perfect. They nag their husbands to bring home the perfect tree and string lights all over the house. They shop till they drop and spend money they don't have. All for what purpose? After all, Christmas is not supposed to be about all the trappings; its purpose is to celebrate the birth of our Savior.

The earth is not going to stop turning on its axis if you don't get that new set of placemats you've been wanting or if the cheese ball you made is not perfectly symmetrical. Stop stressing about minor things and enjoy your life!

"DUST IF YOU MUST"

I don't know who wrote "Dust if you Must," but it emphasizes the importance of keeping our lives in proper priority and not letting life pass us by while we preoccupy ourselves with the unimportant. It is not a license to keep a messy house, but an invitation to relax and enjoy the life God has given us!

"I used to spend at least eight hours every weekend making sure things were perfect in case someone came over. Then one day I realized that no one came over; they were out living life and having fun!

"Now when people visit, I find no need to explain the condition of my home. They are more interested in hearing about the things I have been doing while I was living life and having fun. If you have not figured this out yet, please heed the following advice.

"Life is short. Enjoy it!

"Dust if you must, but wouldn't it be better to paint a picture, write a letter, bake a cake, or plant a seed? We should ponder the difference between want and need.

"Dust if you must, but there is not much time, with rivers to swim, mountains to climb, music to hear, books to read, friends to cherish, and life to lead.

"Dust if you must, but the world is out there with the sun in your eyes, the wind in your hair, a flutter of snow, a shower of rain. This day will not come around again.

"Dust if you must, but bear in mind that old age will come and it is not kind. And when you go – and go you must – you yourself will make more dust!"

THE FUTILITY OF OVERACHIEVEMENT

Psalm 127:2 says, "It is vain for you to rise up early, to sit up late, to eat the bread of sorrows: for so he giveth his beloved sleep." What does this proverb mean?

It means that it is vain – *useless and pointless* – to be stressed, anxious, and always worrying. It is one thing to work to provide for your family and the needs of this life. It is another thing altogether to live with self-imposed stress.

Some people stagger through life pumped up with artificially stimulated energy. They subsist on caffeine and sugar, consuming coffee, sweets, and junk food in large quantities to keep them going from morning till night. They think rest, sleep, and a calm life and demeanor are for underachievers.

"Americans often perceive sleep as a waste of time, a missed opportunity to get more done. We burn the candle at both ends and pride ourselves on all we accomplish, wearing our lack of sleep as a badge of honor. Even though studies prove stress, accidents and health problems increase in direct proportion to our lack of sleep, we're willing to take the risk – because we think we have to produce."[3]

We can expend a lot of energy on things that don't really matter. *When we sacrifice things that matter most – God, family, health, peace – for things that matter least, we should recognize that something is desperately wrong.* We need to evaluate why we are so driven to perfectionism and overachievement.

SELAH

Busyness can be nothing more than a diversion. We keep ourselves busy with things that don't really matter because busyness distracts us from coming face to face with who we really are. For some people, even mundane tasks like mowing and weed eating the lawn can become an obsession.

If we have to stop and be still, then we start thinking. And many people don't want to think about their problems, their issues, and the emptiness in their lives. It seems easier to go, go, go and pretend everything is okay. Busyness becomes a cover-up to keep us from dealing with root issues.

Even though we, at one time, were filled with the Holy Ghost does not mean that we are still *full* of the Holy Ghost. When we are full of the Holy Ghost, God will deal with us to address issues in our lives that need to change. Many times it is easier to fill our lives with useless tasks to cover up our unwillingness to change and the fact that we spiritually running on empty.

Good communication with God and family requires stopping and shutting out distractions. When we don't want to get close to people and God and we don't want to take inventory of our lives, we run, run, run.

We focus on everything in life but what is most important. God. Family. Friends. Our health.

When is the last time you watched a sunset? Took a casual walk with your spouse, holding hands and relaxing together? Spent an afternoon playing games with your children? Prayed and read your Bible? Sat on your back porch and had a long, leisurely chat with a friend?

It has been said that if a man is too busy to pray, he is busier than God ever intended him to be. We must strive to keep first things first.

Selah. Give it a thought. What things are you spending your time on that do not really matter, that only distract you from getting real with God about your life, your struggles, and things in your character that need to change? Why do you involve yourself in the busyness business just for the sake of being busy? Why do you run when God wants you to rest?

Selah. Think about it.

HOPE FOR THE OVERACHIEVER

I am a task-oriented person. I like plans, schedules, and organization. Even in my day-to-day life, I set little goals. Most nights, before I go to sleep, I plan what I am going to do the next day.

I really like the feeling that comes when I accomplish a chore or meet a goal. I like to make lists and I like to mark through the finished tasks.

The good thing about achievement-oriented people is that they get things done. They don't glide through life with unfinished objectives. Give them a target and they will practice until they hit it dead center. Send them on a mission and they will achieve or die trying.

The bad side about achievement-oriented people is that they can get tunnel vision. They think they can do it all and do it all well. They are so driven by their desire to be gratified by achievement that they sometimes misplace their priorities.

I have tried to alter my personality to become more spontaneous and less task-oriented. But I have come to accept that God thinks it is okay that I am the way I am. I don't have to try to artificially morph myself into another personality type. He wants to use me with my personality, not me pretending to be someone else.

But what I have learned to do (and I hope this helps those of you who are also task and achievement-oriented) is to keep my priorities in focus.

When I was writing my first book – *Food for Thought: A Healthy Temple for a Holy God* – I immersed myself into intensive research. Every spare moment was spent studying and processing information about nutrition and health. It was a three-year-long process.

My husband, who provided me with unwavering motivation and support for that first and all subsequent book projects, jokingly says of that time, "I lost my wife for three years." I was very committed to my writing project and from time to time he would have to remind me to come up for air!

Since then, I have tried to temper my intensity by reminding myself that God and family should come first and my achievements second.

If I go-go-go all day long, yet I have neglected prayer, then I have not been successful.

If I am frazzled and stressed out while trying to meet a self-imposed goal, then I have not been successful, despite my accomplishments.

If I neglect other things that are also important, then I have not been successful.

When the Bible refers to temperance, it refers to self-control. Self-control brings balance into our lives. Balance is imperative for goal-oriented people. They must regularly evaluate their position to make sure they don't fall into the abyss that traps many overachievers.

Relax. Get your priorities rearranged. Enjoy your life! God will probably not change your personality and remove your desire to achieve, but He can rescue you from the mentality that equates achievements and busyness with self-worth.

Keep God first in your life. Reliance on your human capabilities will always leave you with a sense of lack and a feeling of emptiness, despite what you achieve. God alone is the Source of your sense of value, worth, and significance.

SWEET SUCCESS

God wants His people to prosper. He wants us to excel at our jobs, He wants our marriages to be healthy and fulfilling, and He wants us to enjoy our lives.

Excelling in a career, perfecting a talent, and earning money are not sinful endeavors. Success is not a sin.

God does not want you to fail. He wants the best for your life.

The following Scriptural passage is lengthy, but consider what God told Joshua: "Every place that the sole of your foot shall tread upon, that have I given unto you, as I said unto Moses.

"Be strong and of a good courage: for unto this people shalt thou divide for an inheritance the land, which I sware unto their fathers to give them.

"Only be thou strong and very courageous, that thou mayest observe to do according to all the law, which Moses my servant commanded thee: turn not from it to the right hand or to the left, that thou mayest prosper whithersoever thou goest.

"This book of the law shall not depart out of thy mouth; but thou shalt meditate therein day and night, that thou mayest observe to do according to all that is written therein: for then thou shalt make thy way prosperous, and then thou shalt have good success" (Joshua 1:3,6-8).

God was referring to not only spiritual blessings, but physical blessings as well. This promise is smack dab in the middle of God's instructions to Joshua about conquering the Promised Land. God wanted to bless the children of Israel, not only with spiritual blessings, but with land. On this land His people would live, grow their food, and raise their children.

The contingent clause of their prosperity was based upon keeping the Word of God foremost in their minds. God wanted to bless them and as long as they kept their focus on Him, the children of Israel would enjoy the fruit of conquest.

God wants us to succeed and do our best, but if He is not at the top of the stack, our success will have a bittersweet flavor. Patrick Morley wrote, "Failure means to succeed in a way that doesn't really matter."[4]

When our desire to be busy relegates God to second place, we have exalted achievement to the place of God. It has become our god.

We can become addicted to busyness. It is easier to *do* than it is to *become*. Rather than *doing*, God wants us to focus more on *being*.

Keep God in the center of all of your endeavors. As you strive to excel in education and business and make financial gains, if God is at the center of your life, you will be able to maintain proper perspective.

If a puzzle is missing one piece, the eye is not drawn to all the pieces that are put together, but the one that is missing. No matter what we accomplish in life, without Jesus in the center of our lives, we are incomplete.

Succeed at what really matters and all other successes will reward you with lasting sweetness, because you will have put God first in all you do.

CHAPTER 4

Stuffed

THE GREAT DECEPTION

To many people, success means having plenty of money in the bank, time for recreation, a nice house, and new cars.

Some find gratification in knowledge and educational achievements.

Still others think success is doing well with their entrepreneurial businesses.

People on the lower end of the social and economic spectrum sometimes envy those with nice clothes, nice cars, and nice homes.

One of the biggest lies Americans are told is that our identity is tied to our secular achievements and our value is equal to our wealth and goods.

A guy could be in debt up to his eyeballs, but if he has a new sports car or pickup truck, people think he is really cool.

A family might always be at odds, with the parents on the verge of divorce, but if they live in a trendy townhouse in an elite part of town, they are presenting an image of normalcy and success.

A teenager who has the most popular and up-to-date technological gadgets feels good about herself.

It is all a lie, a big fat lie, nothing more than a deceptive illusion. People who live with the desire to have more and better stuff will never be content. Lofty ambitions dissolve into empty dreams and the height of prestige brings only disappointment.

People who love stuff always want more stuff…a bigger house, a newer car, and better clothes. They fill their lives with everything except Jesus, so stuff only temporarily satisfies them.

HARMONIOUS HOMES

A harmonious home is not made out of stuff. A fancy house furnished with the finest, most expensive stuff never gave anybody peace.

The writer of Proverbs said that it is better to eat the simplest meal with love, quietness, and harmony than to have a rich, gourmet feast accompanied by discord and strife (Proverbs 15:17; 17:1). After all, what good is an expensive, gourmet meal if the people eating it don't like each other?

Dr. Daniel Segraves writes, "It is love that creates a happy home, not luxury and riches. It is love that makes a dinner a joyous occasion, not the quantity or quality of food. The atmosphere around the table should be one of tranquility and love. Mothers particularly should work at creating an atmosphere of peace for family meals.

"Human reasoning tends to equate an abundance of material things with the quality of life. The Scriptures repeatedly teach the superiority of inner peace over material abundance."[1]

Jesus said, "Lay not up for yourselves treasures upon earth, where moth and rust doth corrupt, and where thieves break through and steal: But lay up for yourselves treasures in heaven, where neither moth nor rust doth corrupt, and where thieves do not break through nor steal: For where your treasure is, there will your heart be also" (Matthew 6:19-21).

"And he said unto them, Take heed, and beware of covetousness: for a man's life consisteth not in the abundance of the things which he possesseth" (Luke 12:15).

Years ago, a popular Christian song reminded us that "the things that matter the most in this world can never be held in our hand."[2]

Wives should not pressure their husbands to buy "stuff" they cannot afford. Do we want our husbands to work overtime to provide stuff for us or do we prefer that they spend that time with our children and us? If our husbands are hard workers and doing all they can to provide for our needs, we should not burden them with guilt, telling them they are not being good enough providers, just because we don't have all the stuff we want and think we need.

Shed the "I want it all and I want it all right now" mindset. Let your husband know that you are satisfied with having him. Any stuff he can provide is simply additional blessings. Take the pressure off of him to provide things that you don't really need and that only create friction in your home. Stuff is not more important than peace and harmony.

A friend of ours told us about how her grandchildren would come to visit. Being normal energetic kids, they would mess up her neat and tidy house during their visits. She would get very frustrated and upset.

Then, the Lord told her that she could always straighten her house when the grandchildren went back to their own home. She needed to enjoy her grandchildren while they were there. By getting so frustrated about her house getting messed up, she was robbing herself of enjoying her time with her family.

Love people more than things. Things are replaceable; people aren't.

GOD'S MEASURE OF SUCCESS

God's measure of success is different from most people's standard. He calibrates things according to a different system.

Jesus spoke a parable about a rich man who was so wealthy that he was going to tear down his old barns and build bigger ones to store all his stuff. God considered that man a fool. Jesus said, "So is he that layeth up treasure for himself, and is not rich toward God" (Luke 12:21). This man was satiated with stuff but spiritually barren.

God measures wealth and success, not according to the brand on your shirt or the amount of money in your IRA, but according to how much you have invested into your heavenly bank account.

During Job's day, success was not measured by Wall Street investments, but by the amount of cattle you owned. By those ancient standards, Job was extremely successful. Job 1:3 reports that Job was "the greatest of all the men of the east."

But Job was successful in another way as well, in the way that really mattered. God came first in his life and Job was spiritually rich.

It is possible to be both monetarily and spiritually rich, as long as priorities are firmly established.

TRUE RICHES

There are a lot of people who, if they examined my life, would not consider me very successful. Since 1999, we have been committed to itinerant ministry, evangelizing for most of those years. We live a transient life that does not enable us to accumulate stuff.

But I don't consider myself deprived or poor. Compared to many Americans, I don't have a lot of stuff, but compared to some people who live in poverty-stricken countries, I am extremely wealthy. I don't think of my life as ascetic and completely non-materialistic; I do like nice things. But when I don't have them, I am content.

For many years, my husband and I have lived in a 5th wheel RV that we pull with a pickup truck. The RV is only a fraction of the size of a house, but it is actually liberating to be relatively stuff-free. Other than our truck and RV, all of our worldly possessions could fit into a 10'x10' space.

I recognize that this lifestyle is not for everyone and I do not consider myself superior to people who like their houses, gardens, and garages full of stuff. The point is that no matter how much stuff we do or don't have, contentment is only found in Jesus, not our possessions. If God ever gives me a lot of money and stuff, I pray that I will continue to keep my focus on Him.

Instead of looking at what you don't have, think about what you do have. If you have Jesus, you are rich.

I do not own a house, but I have a heavenly home being prepared for me (John 14:2-3).

I don't have much money, but I have riches in Heaven (Matthew 6:19-20).

I do not have much stuff, but I have righteousness, peace and joy in the Holy Ghost (Romans 14:17).

I do not have high social status, but pleasing God lets me soar high (Psalm 1:1-3).

If you have Jesus, you are rich in the way that really matters.

COMPARISONS

Advertising bombards kids, convincing them that they need certain "stuff" to fit in with their peers. Kids in turn pressure their parents to provide them with all this stuff.

The ironic thing about giving in to advertising is that the name brand that is popular this year will probably be considered old-fashioned in a decade. Most of the technology that is cutting edge today will be obsolete tomorrow.

Don't measure the success of your life according to what others do or do not have or by what American advertising tells you that you must buy. No matter how we think we measure up – whether better off or less fortunate – when we compare ourselves to others, either outcome will give us an inaccurate perspective of ourselves.

Plus, comparing ourselves to others tends to create envy, which God disapproves of. Proverbs 27:4 says, "Wrath is cruel, and anger is outrageous; but who is able to stand before envy?" If you will resist the temptation to compare yourself to others, you will save yourself a lot of problems.

CONTENTMENT

The weather is too hot…or too cold.
The traffic is too fast…or too slow.
The food is too spicy…or too bland.

On a more serious level, some married people wish they were single and some single people wish they were married.

It seems that a lot of folks spend their entire lives searching for the perfect place, the perfect life, the perfect person to spend their lives with. They seek an elusive pot of gold and an imaginary fountain of youth. Always discontented, they search for things that don't actually exist.

Philippians 4:11 says, "I have learned, in whatsoever state I am, therewith to be content." We have to *learn* to be content; for most people, contentment does not come naturally.

Contentment actually means something different than commonly thought. We tend to believe that discontentment is the result of our lack of certain possessions that we want or think we need. We think, *If I just had more stuff, I would be happy and content.* So we covet more stuff, thinking that once we get enough of what we think we need, then we will be content.

But lack of things does not produce covetousness. Lack of contentment produces covetousness.

Contentment means "Contained within limits; hence, having the desires limited by that which one has; not disposed to repine or grumble; satisfied; contented; at rest."[3]

It seems like an oxymoron: You must use what you already have to limit your desires.

Eve was not content with what she had. Instead, she became fixated on the one thing in the Garden she did not have. She succumbed to the lust of the eyes, lust of the flesh and the pride of life. She was discontent.

I Timothy 6:5-8 talks about people who thought that gain was godliness. Paul then wisely advises Timothy: "But godliness with contentment is great gain. For we brought nothing into this world, and it is certain we can carry nothing out. And having food and raiment let us be therewith content."

In other words, rather than trying to obtain more stuff, be content with what you already have. If you have Jesus, you have more than most people have. Be content with Him.

STRESS-FREE STUFF

In the Bible, owning land, succeeding at business endeavors, and having possessions is never condemned, unless it is obtained and retained at the expense of a relationship with God, family, and personal integrity.

But we can become at ease in Zion (Amos 6:1). In other words, we can be lulled into complacency by our attachment to stuff.

It is okay to own stuff as long as stuff does not own you. Prosperity is great as long as God is not on the back burner of your heart. God wants to be the highest priority in your life, not mixed in with all the stuff in your life.

COMPLETELY CONTENT

When we allow the emptiness back into our hearts because we neglect our relationship with God, we try to fill the void with stuff. We stuff ourselves full of clothes, hobbies, toys, pleasure, and knowledge. We build bigger barns to store our stuff. We tell ourselves that just a little more stuff will bring us contentment and rest.

When we find ourselves becoming discontent, we need to remind ourselves that we are complete in Christ (Colossians 2:10). Hebrews 13:5 says, "Let your conversation be without covetousness; and be content with such things as ye have: for he hath said, I will never leave thee, nor forsake thee." If we have Jesus, we have all we really need.

God would not have told us to be content if it were impossible for us to do so. We have the power to add and subtract things from our lives.

Kept in proper perspective, stuff is good. But God is better…much better!

CHAPTER 5

Play the Game

THE POLLYANNA PLAN

Pollyanna was a fictional heroine born in the imagination of author Eleanor Porter in the early 1900s. The young daughter of a poor missionary, Pollyanna did not live an easy life.

One day, a barrel arrived from the United States and Pollyanna was hoping that the nice people in America had sent her a doll. But instead of finding a doll in the barrel, Pollyanna pulled out a pair of crutches. She was so disappointed.

In spite of her disappointment, Pollyanna's father wanted her to learn to look on the bright side of things. So, pointing to the crutches, he said, "We can be glad that we don't have to use them!"

Thus, the Glad Game was born. No matter how dismal things looked, Pollyanna found something to be thankful about.

Her life became full of joy and she spread this joy to everyone she met. The source of her joy and optimism was her choice to be glad instead of sad. She taught a lot of people how to play the Glad Game and they also learned how to replace complaints with gratitude.

FINDING THE SILVER LINING

For many years, we have traveled from church to church, ministering to people in need. I never cease to find it a little amusing when, as we get ready to leave a church, people make statements like, "It is such a beautiful, sunny day. How nice that you have the day off." I just smile and tell them something like, "Yes, it is a beautiful day."

They have no idea that, by the time we factor in packing, hours of travel (often in hectic traffic), settling in to a new location and unpacking, our "days off" often evolve into 12-16 hour workdays.

I really do love our lifestyle, but it is not a walk in the park. There are a lot of sacrifices involved that people never imagine. Breakdowns on the side of the road. Uncertain income. A life of constant change and adjustment. Weariness. (There have been times I have been so fatigued and worn out that I have cried from exhaustion.)

People only see us arriving at their church with smiles and words of encouragement, preaching, singing, and praying, and then going out to eat with the pastor. This is only about ten percent of our work. The rest is all behind-the-scenes labor that others do not see but that is essential to effectiveness in church services.

Gratitude is one vital ingredient that has pulled me out of many a hole. No matter how bad things get, I try to find something to be glad about. It keeps frustration from overwhelming me. If I look hard enough, I can always find the silver lining in the clouds, no matter how dark the skies are.

TRUCK STOP GRATITUDE

Once, as we were traveling a Mississippi interstate, we stopped at a truck stop to get fuel. It was almost midnight and we were still a long way from our destination. As we pulled up to the pump, we heard a loud and distinct pop. Then we heard another pop. We looked back at our RV and noticed it was leaning to one side. We had not just one flat tire on the RV but two…on the same side.

My husband discovered that we had driven over a piece of metal that had come loose from a tractor-trailer. It had ripped holes in two of our tires.

We were suddenly immobile. The girl working the desk in the truck stop called the manager who took responsibility for the problem, since their maintenance people had not kept the parking lot free of debris. But she could not call her corporate headquarters and ask for permission to help us until the morning.

She told us to leave the RV and truck there for the night and go to a nearby motel. But we could not bring ourselves to leave our truck and RV in the poorly-lit truck stop in case of vandalism. (Because the RV was tilted at an angle, the door would not shut completely and we could not lock it.) So we decided to try to sleep in our RV.

Have you ever tried to sleep on a bed tilted at a 30-degree angle during the stifling, sweltering, oppressive heat of a Mississippi night with the sound of diesel trucks coming and going beside you? Trust me, it is nearly impossible to do, no matter how exhausted you are.

I tried hard to be positive. I wanted a shower, a bed that was not tilted, and to be away from that noisy, smelly truck stop. What to do?

I thought, *Thanks God, this could always be worse. This could have happened to us on the side of a desolate stretch of road. At least, here, I can go into the truck stop to use the restroom and brush my teeth.*

Okay, so my thankfulness was not all that extravagant. But it was thankfulness, nonetheless. I could not find a lot to be thankful about, but even being a little thankful was better than none.

Did being thankful make all my problems go away? Did our tires suddenly inflate? Did the evening become a beautiful 70 degrees?

Not hardly. Our circumstance did not change. But being thankful helped me get through the night without collapsing into despair and frustration.

The next morning, the manager arrived and contacted her corporate headquarters. After quite some time, she was authorized to finance new tires for our RV. Wouldn't you know it that just up the hill, on the same property as the truck stop, was a big rig tire center? Up the hill we went, driving very slowly so we would not damage the rims.

The tire center had to send someone to a nearby town for our tires, since RVs require special tires and they did not have them in stock.

By about noon, the new tires were on our RV and we were pulling back onto the interstate. What we thought would be about a 20-minute stop for fuel had turned into a miserable twelve hours.

But thankfulness pulled us through that hot, dark night…and many more like it. I could replicate this story a hundred times or more, with different scenarios, different states, and different problems. I tell myself, *No matter how bad things are, they could always be worse.*

Thankfulness has become a habit to me. I am not always vocal about it, because I don't want to sound like Miss Goody-Two-Shoes, but inside I always try to find that silver lining. It makes all the difference.

ENTITLEMENT MENTALITY

We live in a thankless world. People feel entitled to things.

While some welfare recipients genuinely need assistance, there are a lot of people who are capable of working but they just won't. They expect the government to pay their rent, electric, water, and sewer bills, and also give them food to eat. Because they have an entitlement mentality, many are not the least bit thankful toward the government and taxpayers who give them a place to live and food to eat. They expect preferential treatment and throw temper tantrums when things don't go their way. People like this rarely express gratitude because they think everyone should be giving to them.

I am highly skeptical of people who come to churches asking for handouts. Of the many people I have encountered through the years who want churches and Christians to give them money, only occasionally is someone genuinely thankful for the help they receive. Many of them expect something for nothing, so to their way of thinking, why should they be thankful?

On the opposite end of the spectrum, I have also known wealthy people who had a similar entitlement mentality. Because of their wealth, they thought people should cater to them. Rather than being thankful for the things people did for them, they felt entitled to special treatment just because they had a bunch of bucks in the bank. Their attitude reeks of self-importance. This type of thinking does not please God any more than that of a very poor person who thinks that the world should give, give, give to him.

As Christians, we can be guilty of adopting an "entitlement mentality" about the things of God. We must be very careful to not take His blessings for granted. Yes, we are His children, but our privileges as children of the Most High are the result of His love and kindness. He rescued us from a miserable life on the streets. We did not rescue ourselves by our own ingenuity or ability.

We do not deserve one thing that God has done for us. When we stop being thankful, we have forgotten where we were when He rescued us. We start thinking that somehow we deserve salvation. We act like we are doing God a favor by living for Him.

Look at all I do for God. He is lucky to have me. The other people in the church should feel fortunate that I am here. Look at my talents and skills.

This is pride. Lack of gratitude stems from pride and pride always leads to destruction (Proverbs 16:18).

If we behave as though we deserve something, then we won't be grateful for it. And lack of gratitude is treacherous waters.

Giving thanks for our food might seem like nothing more than a formality, but it helps us remember that God is the supplier of all good things in our lives, including the food we eat.

Someone said, "Hem your blessings with thankfulness so they don't unravel." If God has blessed you, be thankful. He is the Source of all good things!

THANK GOD

Why should we thank God? First and foremost, because the Bible tells us to, and God always blesses obedience. I Thessalonians 5:18 says, "In every thing give thanks: for this is the will of God in Christ Jesus concerning you."

Being thankful to God is important because it takes our focus off of ourselves and our own problems and hang-ups. Thanksgiving returns our focus to God, where it belongs.

Psalm 69:30 tells us to "magnify him with thanksgiving." When we are grateful to God, He grows bigger and bigger in our minds. He becomes more powerful than anyone or anything else.

Thanksgiving exalts God and His greatness, not circumstances. When we are thankful even in the midst of trying circumstances, we acknowledge that God is bigger than our circumstances. Rather than exalting our problems, we exalt His greatness.

Thankful and content people are sometimes perceived as naïve and simple, not smart enough to analyze events and people and worry about things. Being glad does not mean that we deny the reality of our problems and close our eyes to the facts. It means that we choose to focus on the positives rather than the negatives.

Gratitude cannot be confined to meditation. It needs to be vocalized and expressed in some way.

William Arthur Ward said, "Feeling gratitude and not expressing it is like wrapping a present and not giving it."

Even singing songs of gratitude to God is pleasing to Him. Psalm 147:7 says, "Sing unto the LORD with thanksgiving." When we sing, we use our voices to express our thankfulness to Him. As we sing, we need to not just sing words, but think about the words we are singing and allow gratefulness to flow from our hearts with our words.

Psalm 116:12 poses a question, "What shall I render unto the LORD for all his benefits toward me?" The Psalmist responds with several ways to show our appreciation to God. One of them is simply saying, "Thank you." "I will offer to thee the sacrifice of thanksgiving" (Psalm 116:17).

We can't really give God anything. He already owns it all! But we can surrender our will to Him and we can say, "Thank You."

THANKSGIVING POINTERS

When you begin to pray, the first thing you should do is acknowledge, thank and honor God (Matthew 6:9; Luke 11:2). Don't repent first. Put God's greatness first in your prayer, not your sin. You can take care of your sin after you have exalted the Lord.

Psalm 100:4 instructs us, "Enter into his gates with thanksgiving, and into his courts with praise: be thankful unto him, and bless his name."

Before you could get into the courts of the Tabernacle, you had to walk through a gate. Before you praise God, you must first be thankful.

Thanksgiving is foundational to praise. If we don't begin with thanksgiving, our praise will lack depth. Thank God, not out of duty, but with heartfelt gratitude and sincerity. Thankfulness helps keep your relationship with God alive and fresh.

Be specific when you thank God. Don't just say, "Thank you, Jesus" without any thought behind your words. Tell Him what you are thankful for.

This little poem emphasizes the beauty of being thankful for important things we often take for granted: "For each new morning with its light, For rest and shelter of the night, For health and food, for love and friends, For everything Thy goodness sends."[1]

An old song says, "Count your blessings. Name them one by one."[2] Thank God for life, for clothing, for food, for shelter, for health, for family, for transportation, for freedom, for a job…

Go ahead. Name your blessings. Don't just think about them. Open your mouth and vocalize your thanks for specific blessings in your life. Once you get started, it is hard to know where to stop!

COMPLAINING OR PRAYING?

At times, I have disguised complaining as praying. What I sometimes call prayer, God calls complaining.

Fortunately, He can handle our complaints. He knows that we are only human.

There is, however, a fine line between talking to God about things that are bothering us and becoming obsessed with our complaints. There comes a point when we have to decide if we want to continue being miserable or if we want to cast our cares upon Him.

It is impossible to be thankful and content at the same time you worry and complain. You will either do one or the other, but never both at the same time.

There will never be a shortage of things to complain about. Bad news from the media. Things we don't like about people in our lives – our family, boss, co-workers, even sometimes brothers and sisters in the Lord. Personality conflicts.

Complaining is basically a self-centered response to our immature attitude that wonders, "Why aren't things going the way I want them to? Why aren't people doing things *my* way?"

Complaining has never made problems go away, but prayer and thankfulness keep us focused on the One who has every answer.

I have met people who must enjoy being miserable. They are more comfortable with negativity and complaining than they are with peace. They habitually find things to gripe about. If you talk about positive things around them, they look at you like you are crazy.

But God does not want us to live in a state of constant griping. The reason God hates murmuring and complaining is because it reveals our lack of faith in Him. He is not impressed by whining, but by faith.

Sometimes, grumbling makes perfect human sense. The children of Israel get criticized for murmuring in the wilderness, but I have seen that wilderness, and it is barren, dry, unbelievably hot, and miserable. I really can't blame them for murmuring. I probably would have murmured too. But God wants us to rise above our human mentality to the supernatural realm of faith.

Philippians 4:6 says, "Be careful for nothing; but in every thing by prayer and supplication with thanksgiving let your requests be made known unto God." From beginning to end, encase your prayers in thanksgiving. It will keep you out of complaining mode.

THE PEOPLE PROBLEM SOLVER

Corporations spend a lot of money hiring motivational speakers with the goal of improving morale and work performance and helping people work together harmoniously and productively.

Whether it is at work, at home, at church, or elsewhere, being glad will solve a lot of interpersonal relationship problems, without any expense.

If your spouse's flaws aggravate you, make two lists. First, list the irritating and annoying habits and characteristics of your spouse. Then, list your spouse's good qualities.

The second list will probably be a lot longer than the first list and as you write, your appreciation for your spouse will grow. Sure, he might not be so good at landing his towel in the hamper, but he is a hard worker and a good provider and has a great sense of humor. Little things that get under your skin will fade into the background when you realize that your spouse's good attributes far outweigh the bad.

Are you upset with a sister in the Lord? Do you have a hard time admitting her good traits? In your mind, do her faults stick out like a sore thumb?

You can change your perspective if you will be thankful that your sister is serving God. No, she is not perfect, but she is in the right place to learn and grow.

If you will be glad that at least she is not still wandering in spiritual darkness, you will find yourself loving her instead of resenting her. If you remind yourself that God has brought her this far, you will be encouraged that He will continue to help her change, just as He is helping you.

THANK PEOPLE

Say "Thank You." To your parents. Your children. Your teachers. Your students. Your spouse. Your in-laws. Your brothers and sisters in the Church. A driver who lets you ease in front of him during busy traffic. A clerk at the bakery.

You never know when just smiling at someone and giving him or her a genuine "Thank You" will improve their day. It might even open a door for you to talk to them about the Lord.

There have been times when someone has told me "Thank You" and it has boosted my spirit. I work for the Lord and know that a servant is expected to work without complaining or expecting pats on the back, but "Thank You" is a really nice thing to hear, especially if you think no one noticed what you did.

The Church in Corinth received a letter that contained words of appreciation toward them, a thank you card of sorts. "Ye also helping together by prayer for us, that for the gift bestowed upon us by the means of many persons thanks may be given by many on our behalf" (II Corinthians 1:11).

Some years ago, I was walking out of a store when an older gentleman held the door open for me. I smiled at him and said, "Thank you."

Surprised, he paused and thanked me for allowing him to hold the door for me! He said that a lot of women get offended when he tries to hold the door for them. He actually appreciated the opportunity to be a gentleman for a woman who was not an aggressive I-can-do-everything-myself female with an I-don't-need-a-man mentality.

That was kind of fun. I said "Thank You" and received a "Thank You" in return!

If you are a supervisor, church leader, or music director, don't be afraid to tell people "Thank You" for jobs well-done, their good attitudes and willing hearts. It is okay to acknowledge the good things others do and the contributions they make.

Sometimes, all people need is the expression of a little appreciation. It can make a lot of difference in a relationship, in workplace morale, and in a church.

"God gave you a gift of 86,400 seconds today. Have you used one to say "thank you?"[3] It only takes a second!

WHAT YOU HAVE

I think it would be helpful if every American could visit a third world country. Things that we take for granted are not even options for many people in the world. Accessible medical care. Plenty of food. Education. Houses with air conditioning and heating. A paved and well-posted highway system. Adequate electricity to run our many appliances.

I don't take clean water for granted. I have lived in a developing country, where water is rationed and even that water is not clean according to U.S. standards. After showering in this water, my hair and skin felt greasy. I tried to not think about it too much. To keep from feeling sorry for myself, I've thought, *At least I have water. There are people with large families not far from here who live in tents in the refugee camps. They are allotted very little water, much less than what we have and it is probably not as clean as our water.*

I don't take uncontaminated food for granted. We soaked all of our vegetables in a hydrogen peroxide solution before we could eat them. As we were shopping, I would think, *I know this food is not the best, but at least we have food to eat. Some people in this country would be thrilled if they could buy something other than hummus and pita bread, the cheapest food in the country.*

I don't take a modern washing machine for granted, because for months I used a machine that was just a few steps up from the old washboard method. It was labor intensive and roughened up my hands substantially. As I was spending the better part of a day doing laundry, I would tell myself, *At least I don't have to wash all of these clothes completely by hand.*

I don't take clean air for granted. The air is polluted and for months I felt congestion in my lungs and throat that only went away once I was back in the United States for a while. It was hard to find something to be thankful about when I was hacking and trying to clear my throat and hoping the congestion was not damaging my insides. All I could manage was, *Thanks, God, for helping me through this.*

I'm not trying to make people feel sorry for me. Sacrifice is part and parcel of the missions experience. The rewards of working in missions far outweigh the sacrifices required. But I am reminded of a song I was taught when I was just a Sunday School kid: "Be thankful for the good things that you've got. Be thankful for the good things that you've got. For the good things that you've got are for many just a dream. So be thankful for the good things that you've got."

You don't have to look far to find someone who is in a worse predicament than you. The good things that you've got truly are for many just a dream.

Be thankful. If you have air conditioning in your home, if you have a car to drive, if you have a job, if you have a stove that works, be thankful! Instead of griping about the cons in your life, think about the pros! Even if you are poor by American standards, there are millions of people in the world who would love to trade places with you.

Rather than focusing on what you *don't* have, focus on what you *do* have. If you are thankful, you will discover that there are a lot more good things in your life than bad.

Thanksgiving changes our entire perspective and keeps us from feeling deprived. Thankfulness creates contentment with what we do have, instead of focusing on what we don't have and reinforcing our discontentment.

THE GRATITUDE ATTITUDE

Being glad is like a one-size-fits-all garment. It works for everyone, no matter your plight.

Discouraged? Be glad about something.

Depressed? Thank God for the good things in your life. God does wonderful things for people and they never stop to thank Him. They are miserable because they forget what He has done. One of the quickest ways to pull yourself out of depression and become glad instead of sad is to be thankful.

Struggling with sin and pride? Rid yourself of the entitlement mentality and express gratitude to God and people.

Negative and self-centered? Think about the goodness of the Lord and you will find yourself becoming less self-centered and more God-centered.

Someone said, "Gratitude is the best attitude." Why? Because your attitude affects your altitude.

Thankfulness is not something we should do only now and then. It should be a way of life. This is not just positive thinking; it is biblical thinking.

Some of you might remember when churches used to have "testimony services." During these times, people could stand and tell everyone about the good things God had done for them. These corporate times of thanksgiving were always encouraging.

Even though most churches don't still have "testimony services," we can tell others about the goodness of the Lord during casual conversations while we are standing in line at the bank or grocery store, in the foyer of the church, or while eating at a restaurant.

It is good to tell others about what God has done for you. It will encourage them and it will encourage you.

BE EXCEEDING GLAD

The point of Pollyanna's Glad Game is not to play it only when life is perfect. If that were so, the Glad Game would never be taken out of the box, because life will never be perfect.

Don't wait for your circumstances or life to change before you are thankful. Find something to be thankful about even when things aren't going good.

The Bible uses the phrases "Be glad" and "Rejoice," sometimes in the same verse.

The passage containing these phrases that I find most striking is Matthew 5:12. Right in the middle of Jesus telling His disciples that they would be persecuted, He said, "Rejoice, and be exceeding glad: for great is your reward in heaven."

Wow. Even in the midst of physical persecution, God wants us to "Rejoice, and be exceeding glad." Not just glad, but "*exceeding* glad!"

This is serious stuff. Rejoicing, being glad and thankful, even in the worst of times, is an antidote worth using.

If you want a joy-filled life, activate your gratitude. Be thankful. Celebrate the good things in your life.

Play the Glad Game! Be glad. Rejoice!

CHAPTER 6

Worry Remedy

WHAT IS WORRY?

Webster's Dictionary says worry means "to feel or express undue care and anxiety."[1]

To some people, it is a foreign thought that God wants them to have a worry-free life. Worry is so ingrained into their thought processes that they can't imagine life without it. To them, worry is a completely natural and justifiable response to, well, just about anything.

There is good news for worriers: There will never be a shortage of things to worry about. If they just let their minds wander a little, they will find something to latch onto with enthusiastic, energy-draining worry.

Advise worriers to quit worrying and get ready for a fight. Worry has become their raggedy security blanket and they'll defend their right to worry with gusto.

But if we want to live a peaceful Christian life, the habit of worrying becomes problematic. Why?

Because worry and peace are non-reconcilable enemies.

PRICELESS PEACE

Peace.

Everybody wants it. Few have it.

Because peace is so rare, people think it has an expensive price tag.

Isaiah 9:6 reveals that the Messiah would be known as the "Prince of Peace." Princes have power. This Prince of Peace has power to dispense to people all the peace they need.

Though Jesus the Messiah came so that every person on earth could have peace, not many people receive His peace. Instead, they live with fear, worry, and anxiety. Even many Christians do not know God as their Prince of Peace.

Why do people choose anxiety instead of peace? The reason is simple: In order for the Prince of Peace to rule your life, you have to submit to His authority.

Worry is a feeble and ineffective attempt to control circumstances and people. The reason worriers worry is because they don't like not being in control. Worriers think that if they worry enough, they can change people and circumstances. When I begin to worry, it should be a red flag signifying to me that I am futilely attempting to control a person or situation.

Desire for control has its root in fear so, simply, *worry is faith in fear*. It is impossible to worry and pray the prayer of faith at the same time. When we worry, we put more faith in our fears than we do in God.

If you will realize that God is in control, you won't feel anxious when things happen that are beyond your ability to control. You won't feel the need to control, i.e., worry.

So, yes, peace is expensive. We have to take our hands off the wheel and let God drive. We have to learn to sit in the back seat and enjoy the drive and not worry about anything at all.

But peace is also priceless. Because once we have it, we love it, and we don't want to sell it for any price. When we realize that in order to worry, we have to sell our peace, we shut the door in worry's face.

PRAYER FOCUS

Worry focuses on a problem. As long as we focus on the problem, God's hands are tied. Until we loosen our grip on the problem and quit trying to fix it ourselves, God cannot work.

Sometimes, we talk more about the problem than the Problem Solver. We are better acquainted with the problem than we are with the Problem Solver.

Philippians 4:6-7 says, "Be careful for nothing; but in every thing by prayer and supplication with thanksgiving let your requests be made known unto God. And the peace of God, which passeth all understanding, shall keep your hearts and minds through Christ Jesus."

Prayer is one of the key ways that we build and maintain our relationship with God. As our relationship with God grows, we will enjoy more and more peace.

Prayer is the best stress management technique. If we pray with thankfulness, the peace of God will guard our hearts and minds through Christ Jesus. If we pray rather than worry, our hearts and minds will be anxiety-free!

"And this is the confidence that we have in him, that, if we ask any thing according to his will, he heareth us: And if we know that he hear us, whatsoever we ask, we know that we have the petitions that we desired of him" (I John 5:14-15).

These verses do *not* say, "If we *worry*, He hears us." Rather, when we *pray*, He hears us.

PERSONAL PEACE

It is possible to have personal peace in the midst of social unrest.

When my husband and I travel to the Middle East to live and minister, we pray about the right time to go and how long we should stay.

Since we know that we are right where God wants us, we use caution while we are there but we are not afraid.

During one of our stays in the Middle East, we lived in a Jordanian town close to the Syrian border. The Syrian war was in full swing and bombs frequently exploded about ten miles away, in Dara'a, Syria.

We gave Bible studies and oversaw a church in a city called Zarqa, known as a breeding ground for terrorists.

We drove dark stretches of road that might have been dangerous if our car became disabled and people with the wrong motives saw us stranded.

When we lived in Jerusalem, Israel, we were well aware that violent conflict between Palestinians and Israeli Jews could spark at any time.

We knew better than our friends and family back home just how volatile and potentially dangerous our situation was. But we did not allow fear to take root in us.

I appreciate the concern friends and family express about our safety. But when someone says, "I am so worried about you," I cringe inside. I honestly don't want anyone to worry about me. I want people to care about us, yes, but not worry. Worry is so unproductive.

What I usually say in response is, "Please don't worry about us. God will take care of us. Just keep us in your prayers." If I can encourage people to pray for us instead of worry, I know that we have one more prayer partner on board with us.

7 GOOD REASONS TO DITCH WORRY

#1. *Worry produces anxiety.*

Whenever I begin to feel anxious about something, my anxiety is a symptom telling me that I am feeling out of control. We need to use our anxiety as a Check Engine light. Anxiety signifies that we need to stop, regroup, and remind ourselves that God is big enough to handle our biggest problems.

Anxiety is a peace-thief. Ask God to help you *rest in Him*!

#2. *Worry is not a virtue.*

I have never noticed "worry" nestled among the lists of the Gifts or the Fruit of the Spirit. Yet, some people think their official job in the Church is to worry. Some people take this approach: "Other people can pray and trust in God. I'll do all the worrying."

Prayer and worry are not the same thing. There is nothing virtuous, holy, or godly about worrying.

#3. *Worry is not of God*!

As has already been stated, worry comes from a desire to control. Desire for control is rooted in insecurity and fear.

Replace your fear with trust in God.

#4. *Worry does not work.*

Worry does not get the job done. It only interferes with our effectiveness.

#5. *Worry is disguised doubt.*

It is impossible to worry and have faith at the same time. If you doubt and worry, you will be overwhelmed. If you place your faith and trust in God, you'll have peace.

Doubt and worry do not please God; faith pleases God (Hebrews 11:6). God does not respond to worry; God responds to faith.

#6. *Worry presupposes things that rarely happen.*

Someone said, "I know worrying works because almost everything I worry about never happens."

Worry preys on our imagination. Its fertile ground is "What Ifs?" that rarely materialize. At times I have found myself a bundle of nerves, uptight about situations that eventually work out just fine. The older I get, the more I realize that when you live for God, things have a way of working out.

#7. *Worry robs you of precious time.*

Corrie ten Boon wrote, "Worry does not empty tomorrow of its sorrow, it empties today of its strength." Why waste precious moments of our lives worrying – often about things that are completely unwarranted – when we can enjoy a life of simple, childlike trust and faith?

We need to take this approach: I might cry tomorrow; I don't know what tomorrow holds. But today all is well. I'm going to smile and enjoy this day of life Jesus has given me. I will not cloud today's sunshine with tomorrow's worries. I will not fabricate fear and negativity.

Anyone who dwells on the negatives in life is going to be miserable. Why waste time anticipating the bad? As LaJoyce Martin said, "Bad times will manufacture themselves. If we're going to have good times, we must manufacture them ourselves in our own Good Times Factory."

REST IN PEACE

Do you have trouble sleeping because you are worrying and fretting? Read and believe Proverbs 3:24: "When thou liest down, thou shalt not be afraid: yea, thou shalt lie down, and thy sleep shall be sweet."

And Psalm 4:8: "I will both lay me down in peace, and sleep: for thou, LORD, only makest me dwell in safety."

If, during the day, you will keep your mind on God, you will have less trouble at night. Isaiah 26:3-4 says, "Thou wilt keep him in perfect peace, whose mind is stayed on thee: because he trusteth in thee. Trust ye in the LORD for ever: for in the LORD JEHOVAH is everlasting strength."

With a God who has "everlasting strength," why not rest instead of worry? It sounds like God is big and strong enough to handle every problem in our lives. No matter how big our problems seem to us, they are not too big for God.

REST IN THE TEST

I once saw a sign with the following message: "Good morning! This is God. I will be handling all of your problems today and I will not be needing your help. So have a good day!" *If God is not worried, then why should I be?*

One of the keys to successful Christian living is learning to not carry things that are too heavy for us. "Casting all your care upon him; for he careth for you" (I Peter 5:7). "Casting" means "to throw upon."

Draw close to Jesus, close enough that you can cast all your cares upon Him. In His presence, He will lighten your load and ease your anxieties.

Peace comes from giving to God what is too heavy for us to handle. You can have peace even if bad things are happening if you let the Prince of Peace take care of what you cannot.

Every burden that God wants us to carry will never be too heavy if we are yoked together with Him. He does most of the pulling!

Matthew 11:28-30 is a beautiful invitation from Jesus: "Come unto me, all ye that labour and are heavy laden, and I will give you rest. Take my yoke upon you, and learn of me; for I am meek and lowly in heart: and ye shall find rest unto your souls. For my yoke is easy, and my burden is light."

When Jesus steps to the bow of your boat, your stress will become rest. "And he arose, and rebuked the wind, and said unto the sea, Peace, be still. And the wind ceased, and there was a great calm" (Mark 4:39).

THE RESTORATION OF REST

I have been in situations where I was not filled with peace, but worry, despair, and fear. I looked at the situations and people involved and said to myself, "I am upset because of them and their actions. I am worried and confused because of this circumstance."

Over time, I learned that my reasoning was faulty. Nobody can cause me to be fearful without my permission. Nobody can make me worry. I *choose* to worry.

The level of my peace is a product of my own choices. I alone have the power to decide whether I will worry or let God's peace comfort and assure me.

I am responsible for my own peace. I choose to worry or choose to allow God to become my Prince of Peace.

Worry is a choice. Just because a person is not absorbed with worry does not mean that her life is perfect. It means she has chosen to not worry.

Worry-free people are easy to be around. They bring calm to people who are agitated and help stabilize difficult situations.

WORRY REMEDY: PEACE

Jesus said, "Peace I leave with you, my peace I give unto you: not as the world giveth, give I unto you. Let not your heart be troubled, neither let it be afraid" (John 14:27).

If you have the Comforter in your life, you have the power to live every day with peace, not fear. You can choose to trust and not worry.

Finally, let's take direction from one more encouraging Scripture: "And let the peace of God rule in your hearts, to the which also ye are called in one body; and be ye thankful" (Colossians 3:15).

Let the Prince of Peace rule your heart and mind. You won't be sorry!

The LORD will give strength unto his people;
the LORD will bless his people with peace.

Psalm 29:11

CHAPTER 7

Fear's Worst Nightmare

PHOBIC FEAR

People have all kinds of fears.

"I'm afraid of heights."

"I'm afraid of thunderstorms."

"I'm afraid of being alone."

"I'm afraid of getting cancer."

"I'm afraid my child will ruin his life."

"I'm afraid I will lose my job."

"I'm afraid I will fail."

"I'm afraid someone will ridicule me."

"I'm afraid my husband will leave me."

"I'm afraid…" "I'm afraid…" "I'm afraid…"

These days, people tend to label fears as "phobias." Some say, "I have a phobia" in the same way we might say, "I have a cold." "Having a phobia" makes fear sound clinical and almost normal.

Labeling fear a phobia can make fear seem justifiable and minimize the real control it has over our lives.

DEFENSE MECHANISM

Fear is an instinctive self-protective mechanism. Fear is what we feel when we are about to have a car accident or we are on the verge of falling off the edge of a cliff. It is what we feel when a loved one abandons us, when the economy crashes, and when we lose a job.

Although fear is a natural response, when we allow it to dominate our lives, it is a cruel master. It can be merciless. Fear paralyzes faith. If allowed to rule our hearts and minds, fear leads to desperation, irrational behavior, and hopelessness.

IMPRISONED BY FEAR

Some fears are relatively insignificant, such as "I'm afraid of ants." Other fears are debilitating, like "I'm afraid of rejection."

Usually, fear is the product of past experiences or exposure. For example, some people fear flying in airplanes because of news reports about plane crashes. Some people are afraid that they will get a certain disease, because their family members have had that disease.

Often, people are fearful because they have been hurt by past relationships and are afraid to trust anyone.

They expect people to hurt them. Even when they meet people who are kind to them, they keep them at arm's length because they are fearful of being hurt again. Often, fear causes people to lash out at others with harsh, angry words. In the process, some try to gain the upper hand and use these angry words to put up walls of protection.

When people feel like their lives and circumstances are out of their control, they work hard to try to gain control, usually without success. It is a miserable round-robin cycle that does not seem to have an exit door.

They build walls around their hearts that they think will protect them from being hurt again. These walls prevent them from giving and receiving love.

They are imprisoned by fear. They have willingly walked into their self-made prison and chosen to live there.

FEAR-FREE

People in the Bible were human just as we are. They experienced fear just as we do.

But over and over and over again, God encouraged His people to not be afraid. To Abram, Isaac, Jacob, Hagar, Joshua, Gideon, Daniel, Zacharias, Mary, Peter, Jairus, Paul, John, and others He said, "Fear not."

How could God say that? Didn't He know the desperate situations some of these people were facing?

To us, when things are out of our control, fear seems like the perfectly natural, normal, and logical response.

But God sees the big picture and He knows that if we will simply trust Him instead of being fearful, He will take care of everything.

God would not have told Isaac, Joshua, and Paul to not fear if it were an impossible thing to do.

The reality is that, in God's kingdom, people who choose to reject fear's prison bars are not living in a fantasy world. Rather, they are living the way God wants them to live: Fear-free.

CONFRONTING FEAR

In a Christian's life, fear has no validity or usefulness. We need to acknowledge and identify our fear, then face it head-on with the Word of God. This confrontation requires that we identify the root of our fear.

It has been said that if we don't conquer our fear, it will conquer us. Fear will hold us captive as long as we allow it to.

For the believer, fear is a fate worse than death. Fear can become as debilitating as the most crippling disease.

We alone have the power to choose to either simply believe God and His promises or believe fear's debilitating lies.

Intimidation and fear are first cousins. Someone said, "You cannot intimidate me without my permission." Neither can fear continue to rule our lives unless we allow it to. Through the infilling of the Holy Spirit, God has empowered us with the ability to overcome fear.

THE SOLUTION

If we are fearful, it is not the Spirit of God that gave us the fear. Instead of fear, God gives people wonderful things like power, love and a sound mind (II Timothy 1:7).

How do we defeat fear? By changing the way we think? By having more faith?

Our mindset and faith are important elements in overcoming fear, but they are not the complete solution.

The primary weapon we use to defeat fear is love. Love is a fruit of the Spirit (Galatians 5:22). As we allow God's Spirit to work in our lives and cultivate in us His love, fear will begin to lose its power over us.

I John 4:18 says, "There is no fear in love; but perfect love casteth out fear: because fear hath torment. He that feareth is not made perfect in love."

"Perfect love casteth out fear."

As we allow God to cultivate the fruit of love in our lives, that love will overcome fear.

But in and of itself, the love of God is not fear's worst nightmare.

- When you refuse to confine God's love to ink on the pages of your Bible…
- When you no longer allow God's love to stay one-dimensional in your life…
- When God's love becomes something more than a dutifully quoted John 3:16…
- When the demonstration of God's love on a distant cross 2,000 years ago becomes to you more than a historical record…
- When you acknowledge that God does not just love everyone else, but He loves you too…
- When God's love becomes a reality in your mind and life…
- When you allow God's love to penetrate your mind and heart enough that you trust Him more than fear…

…then fear doesn't stand a chance.

WHAT FRIGHTENS FEAR

What fear dreads most is *you understanding and believing* that God loves you and that you can trust Him with your entire life. That is fear's worst nightmare.

As your relationship with God continues to grow, as your realization of His love for you becomes greater, and as you learn to give away the love you have received, fear will vanish. You will relinquish your fears, replacing them with trust.

We believe in God but we are afraid to trust Him because we do not have a healthy understanding of how much He loves us. He is not out to hurt us, but to help us. He is our friend, not our enemy.

A SAFE PLACE

When I was a child, our church was across a busy street from a parking lot where my parents parked their car. I can remember being in my dad's arms as we crossed that busy street. I was never afraid, although I was aware of all the traffic and commotion. I knew my dad loved me and would keep me safe if his very life depended upon it. I could trust him.

When a child knows that her parent loves her, she feels secure and safe. She knows that her parent loves her enough to protect her. So the child is content. She trusts her parent.

When we are fearful, it is because we have not been "made perfect in love."

Are you putting more trust in your fears than you are putting in God? Does your love need to be perfected? Does the story of Calvary need to become a reality in your life?

David said, "What time I am afraid, I will trust in thee" (Psalm 56:3). "In God have I put my trust: I will not be afraid what man can do unto me" (Psalm 56:11).

You are safe in your Father's care. He will protect you. You can trust Him.

GOD'S PERFECT LOVE

These awesome revelations about God's love for you deepen as a result of thankfulness. In other words, as you rehearse in your mind and vocalize the good things God has already done for you, you become more aware of His tender mercies and His loving kindness towards you.

The closer you get to Jesus, the more you will learn how much He loves you. His love will give you security and remove your fears. As you spend more time in His presence, you will find your fears dissipating.

When you feel God's protective arms around you during times of prayer, you will find the security you need. The Spirit of love will combat the spirit of fear and displace apprehension and anxiety.

You will never defeat fear on your own. "Perfect love casteth out fear" and God is that perfect love. The more you understand God's love toward *you*, the less fear you will have.

That understanding is fear's worst nightmare.

CHAPTER 8

Losing Your Mind

THE REAL DEAL

While attending Bible College, I often had early morning classes taught by an inspiring lady of prayer and faith.

At 7 a.m., when most of us girls were still half asleep and in need of toothpicks to keep our eyes open, she would enter the classroom with a big smile.

"Good morning, girls! Isn't this a beautiful day?"

Most of us had probably not yet noticed whether the day was beautiful or not, but our enthusiastic instructor had noticed. She always talked about good things. She radiated joy and life.

One day, a friend of mine and I were talking about school and our conversation turned to her.

"Do you think she's for real?" my friend skeptically asked.

"Yeah," I said, "I think she's for real."

We both pondered that for a while. I thought, *I wonder if I could be like that someday. Full of faith and bringing cheer and hope to everyone I meet.*

POSITIVES AND NEGATIVES

Before you inwardly groan and think, *Yet another book about positive thinking*, read on. It so happens that the Bible has a lot to say about this subject, so it must be pretty important to God.

The words "positive" and negative" are not found in the Bible, at least, not in the King James Version. But extreme opposites in a human's thoughts, behavior, and speech are displayed by dramatic words like "good and evil" and "life and death."

In addition to the Bible, examples of extreme opposites of positives and negatives can be found in many things in life, including mathematics.

In mathematics, there are positive numbers and negative numbers. Positive numbers are numbers above 0. Negative numbers are numbers below 0. An example of a positive number is: The temperature is 20 degrees above 0. An example of a negative number is: The temperature is 20 degrees below 0. Positive and negative numbers are considered opposites.

Just as in mathematics, the Bible presents positives and negatives as a natural part of the way things work. Positives and negatives are necessary because they indicate that we are not robots, but people equipped with the power to choose.

Since the time when God placed the Tree of Knowledge of Good and Evil in the Garden of Eden, we have had the power to choose. Yes, God forbade Adam and Eve to eat the fruit from that tree, but He let them make their own choice.

OPTIONS

In a sense, the Bible can actually be viewed as a negative book. Surprised?

Think about this: The Bible is a book of extremes. For example, consider Romans 11:22, "Behold therefore the goodness and severity of God: on them which fell, severity; but toward thee, goodness, if thou continue in his goodness: otherwise thou also shalt be cut off."

Goodness. Severity.

Opposites.

One positive. One negative.

Some people experience the severity of God, others, His goodness.

Some see the Bible's positives. Others see its negatives. It contains both. Because of its divinely arranged positives and negatives, the Bible is actually a perfectly balanced book.

How we respond to the Bible's instructions for our lives will determine whether we think of the Bible as repulsive and negative or beautiful and positive.

To the children of Israel, Moses said, "I call heaven and earth to record this day against you, that I have set before you life and death, blessing and cursing: therefore choose life, that both thou and thy seed may live" (Deuteronomy 30:19).

It's another way of saying that we decide if we will have positive or negative lives. Being able to choose between "life and death, blessing and cursing" is good, because it means we are free to determine our own path.

THE CHOICE IS YOURS

People get angry with God and blame Him when bad things happen in their lives.

God gets blamed for a lot of things He does not do. When people hurt us, we take it out on God, but it was not Him who hurt us! Just as God does not stop us when we hurt people, He does not stop others when they hurt us because every human being has been given the power of choice.

Sometimes we blame God for problems that we create on our own. And some things are just life.

People these days seem to think that their lives should be rosy without any effort on their part. They seem to think that just because they breathe air, they should be blessed in every way.

That thought completely opposes the teachings of the Bible. In the Bible, *we* are the ones responsible for our level of joy, peace, and contentment. God's blessings are readily available, but we must activate them through belief, humility, and life application. The entire book of Proverbs and almost the entirety of the Epistles tell us what to do if we want to be blessed.

A successful life is not the same thing as a trouble-free life. Being successful does not mean that you will not have family troubles or never get sick.

You won't find a single example of a person in the Bible who was greatly used of God that did not experience troubles. In fact, for many of them, troubles were the impetus that caused them to turn to God and develop a relationship with Him or the catalyst that helped them fulfill God's purpose for their lives.

Glorious Christian living is not achieved when our lives are free of problems. It is achieved when we focus on the Hope we have. The day we stop expecting everything in life to be perfect is the day we start living realistically.

Some people waste their entire lives resenting God for bad things that happen to them. Instead of blaming God, we need to take a "Where to from here" approach. *Okay, so I got a raw deal. Now what? God will help me. I don't have to drown in despair.*

God never promised us a problem-free life. In fact, for most people, life is one crisis after another. Everyone has problems and challenges. We all get thrown a lot of curve balls that we were not anticipating. We won't always live on Easy Street. It is unrealistic to think that we should be exempt from trouble and anything adverse.

But one thing we can count on. God never changes. He is a Rock that cannot be moved. He will be our stability when everything else is topsy-turvy. For every negative, there is a positive. We are not exempt from trials, but He has a promise to accompany every trial.

For every weapon that is formed against us, God has an effective counter-attack weapon. Isaiah 54:17 promises, "No weapon that is formed against thee shall prosper." God did not say that weapons would never be used against us. He said that they would not prosper. At our disposal is the whole armor of God that is capable of defeating every enemy (Ephesians 6:10-17).

The beautiful thing about the choices God gives us is that a negative is rarely presented in the Bible without a positive answer, hope, and promises accompanying it.

The choice is yours.

CHOOSE THE POSITIVES

We may not be able to control the environment we live in, but we can create an atmosphere of peace and joy within us.

You could live in poverty or be surrounded by luxury. You could have a pleasant family or a not-so-pleasant family. You could live in a country of religious freedom or a country of religious oppression.

Externals determine the level of opposition we will have in our lives. The more opposition, the more challenges we will encounter. But every challenge can be more than adequately met with the power of God on our side.

We can live surrounded by poverty and not allow ourselves to be overwhelmed by despair. Family members may routinely speak negatively, but we can choose to be positive. Through the ages, Christians have survived – at times, thrived – in countries that opposed Christianity.

I love the promise of II Corinthians 4:8-9. "We are troubled on every side, yet not distressed; we are perplexed, but not in despair; Persecuted, but not forsaken; cast down, but not destroyed."

There they are again: Positives and negatives. But the negatives are nearly buried by the awesome positives!

NPV

One of the key factors that enable us to excel in the midst of adverse circumstances is found in our power to choose what we think about. What we think about will determine our direction.

From the NPV, we read Philippians 4:8. "Finally, brethren, whatsoever things are false, whatsoever things are shameful, whatsoever things are unjust, whatsoever things are filthy, whatsoever things are hateful, whatsoever things are of bad report; if there be any immorality, and if there be any criticism, think on these things."

If you noticed that this verse reads a bit different from other Bible translations, remember that we quoted from the NPV (Negative Person's Version).

This is my tongue-in-cheek attempt to emphasize how we can read the Word, yet not really believe it and apply it to our own lives. There is no actual translation called the NPV, but our thoughts and speech seem to indicate that we think there is.

The actual rendering of Philippians 4:8 tells us to think about things that are true, honest, just, pure, lovely, and of good report. When we allow our minds to instead think about things that are false, shameful, unjust, filthy, hateful, and of bad report, we are disobeying the Word of God and hurting ourselves in the process.

Some Christians are consumed with gnawing negativity and infected with poisonous pessimism. The NPV is their go-to translation. If the topic of a conversation is negative, they are eager to jump right in and join the discussion. They'll grasp at straws just to have something negative to say.

Habitually negative people have low levels of faith. Negativity alters our perception to such an extent that God's ability seems weak and ineffectual in contrast to people, problems, and obstacles in our lives.

Quit reading from your Negative Person's Version. It will only give you a dreary life.

Choose instead the pure Word of God, filled with promises of peace if we think about things that are true, honest, just, pure, lovely, and of good report.

Biblical thinking is not just a positive mental attitude that some psychologists consider the cure-all for people's lives. Yes, biblical thinking is positive, but it is God-based thinking. Our faith rests in God and our thoughts focus on God's greatness and power.

When our faith rests in God, we think and speak words of hope. We edify people instead of discourage them. We believe in the power of God to transform anyone, no matter who they are or what they have done.

This God-focus translates to a life of victory, peace, and triumph. It is a glorious way to live.

GATEKEEPERS

Proverbs 23:7 says, "As he thinketh in his heart, so is he."

The Hebrew word used here for "thinketh" means "to act as a gatekeeper" and "to estimate, to calculate." In the Bible, doorkeeper, porter, and gatekeeper are interchangeable words.

- Gatekeepers guarded the gates of cities and private homes. They opened and closed the gates at appropriate times.

- Levites were appointed to guard the Temple gates (I Chronicles 9:23-27).
- Gatekeepers lived near the temple and had charge of the freewill offerings (II Chronicles 31:14).
- Gatekeepers prevented anything unclean from entering the house of the Lord (II Chronicles 23:19).

MENTAL FILTRATION SYSTEM

Furnaces have filters. Cars have fuel and oil filters. Some people install air filters in their homes. The purpose of a filter is to keep the bad from affecting the good.

Essentially, this is the gatekeeper concept of the Bible. Although a gatekeeper had multiple responsibilities, probably his most important job was protecting what was within the walls and gates of the city or Temple.

A gatekeeper would not refuse one enemy, then allow the next enemy who came along to enter the city. No, *all* enemies were refused. A gatekeeper knew that if he allowed an enemy to enter the city, the enemy would destroy the people inside.

I Corinthians 6:19 tells us that our bodies are temples of the Holy Ghost. Because we realize that our bodies house the Spirit of God, many of us take responsibility for our spiritual health. We pray, read the Bible, and receive teaching and instruction from pastors and evangelists.

We also take responsibility for our physical health by exercising and eating properly. We want to be good stewards of God's house.

We also need to remind ourselves that our minds are God's minds. We should be good stewards of our minds. We should reject any thoughts or words that are spoken to us that contradict the Word of God. We should not allow such words and thoughts to lodge in our minds. Because we are temples of God's Spirit, we need to be gatekeepers of our minds, taking responsibility for our spiritual, mental, and emotional health.

Philippians 4:8 provides us with a filtering guide for our minds. Before we allow ourselves to dwell on any one thought, we must ask, "Does this thought pass through each of the gates of Philippians 4:8?" If not, then we must banish it from our minds and replace it with an acceptable thought.

Before you allow a thought to ferment in your mind, ask yourself if it is an enemy or friend. Will it hurt you or help you?

Use the following guide to help you determine if a thought is safe or harmful.

- *"True" means "accurate, certain, reality, factual."*

Does this thought accurately portray the truth about the situation? Do I know all there is to know so that I can draw a factual conclusion? Am I intentionally concealing some facts so I can justify my thoughts?

- *"Honest" means "honorable (to esteem), venerable (to reverence, worship, adore)."*

Does this thought honor God? Am I showing reverence to God by allowing this thought in my mind? Does this thought bring honor to others?

- *"Just" means "equitable in character or action (equal in regard to the rights of persons); distributing equal justice; fair; impartial."*

Does this thought show partiality to any party involved? Am I biased in my judgment?

(Note: There are three sides to every story. For example, in a marital conflict, there is his side, her side, and the truth. We would do well to withhold judgment unless we know all the facts.)

- *"Pure" means "clean, chaste, innocent, modest."*

Are my thoughts clean, holy, and pure? Would I feel ashamed if others knew what I was thinking about?

- *"Lovely" means "acceptable, pleasing."*

Are my thoughts pleasing and acceptable to God?

- *"Of good report" means "well spoken of, reputable."*

Is this thought a good report? When my thought becomes words, does it give the hearer joy or sorrow? Does it encourage or discourage the hearer? Does it add to or detract from my life and the lives of others?

No one in their right mind would see a home intruder trying to break into their home and open the door and welcome him in. Consider unwholesome thoughts home invaders and guard against them.

Most of the places we lived in the Middle East had walls and gates around the buildings for security. In the United States, people use advanced security systems, multiple locks, motion sensor lights, and even old-fashioned peepholes to notify them of unwanted intruders.

Just as homes have security systems and alarms, we can use the Spirit and Word of God to put us on high alert if an evil thought tries to barge its way into our minds. If we guard our minds, we won't have to try later to disarm and remove evil thoughts that want to destroy us.

Be a vigilant gatekeeper of your mind. Filter out the bad, let in the good!

ANTICIPATING THE POSITIVE

A woman I met had breast cancer. Her mother had it as well. This woman's sister, who does not have breast cancer, said that she was considering having a mastectomy.

She was anticipating getting cancer and thought that she might as well get a mastectomy before she got cancer so she wouldn't have to do it later.

This lady's train of thought horrified me.

But how many times in my life have I looked at situations and anticipated a mess when God wanted me to see a miracle in the making?

When I meet someone new, is my first inclination to see their faults or their strong points? When I hear about a terrible sickness in someone's life, do I immediately feel hopeless or do I remember that God's power is great enough to heal anything? Do I try to correct unhealthy relationships on my own or do I leave them in God's hands and let Him work them out?

Someone said, "Setbacks are God's setups for a miracle." Is your glass half full or half empty? Do you anticipate the negative or the positive?

REPLACEMENT SURGERY

When our minds try to control us with evil thoughts, we need to give them something else to think about. We should train our minds through the power of the Holy Ghost to not dwell on sinful thoughts. We should fill our minds with the Word, forcing evil thoughts out of our minds and replacing them with good thoughts.

Feed your mind good things. Replace thoughts and words of negativity, fear, and unbelief with positive, uplifting, encouraging words of faith and optimism. Use Bible language instead of carnal language.

Instead of thinking, "My situation will never change" say "With God, all things are possible. I'm putting my trust in God to work this situation out."

Instead of thinking "I'll always struggle with this sin. I will never overcome" say "I can do all things through Christ who strengthens me."

Instead of thinking, "My sickness will kill me. I have no hope" say "With Jesus, there is always hope. I am putting my faith and trust in Him."

VICTIM TO VICTOR

People involved in ministry usually want better for people than they want for themselves. One of the greatest ministry challenges is helping people believe that God really does want them to enjoy victorious abundant life.

Too many people consider themselves victims of their pasts and circumstances. They think they will never overcome. They think that some things in their lives will never change.

You cannot simultaneously have an overcomer and victim mentality. If you are a child of God, you should no longer consider yourself a victim.

Trials and obstacles do not mean that God does not love us! They are in our lives to draw us close to Him and help us grow.

The next time the enemy tells you that you are a victim, listen instead to what God has to say about you:

"Who shall separate us from the love of

Christ? shall tribulation, or distress, or persecution, or famine, or nakedness, or peril, or sword?

"Nay, in all these things we are more than conquerors through him that loved us.

"For I am persuaded, that neither death, nor life, nor angels, nor principalities, nor powers, nor things present, nor things to come, Nor height, nor depth, nor any other creature, shall be able to separate us from the love of God, which is in Christ Jesus our Lord" (Romans 8:35,37-39).

Did you get that? Do you realize just how binding God's love is for you? You are not a victim. You are a victor.

More accurately, you are not just a conqueror; you are *more* than a conqueror through Christ!

FROM A POSITIVE POINT OF VIEW

Certainly, from time to time, we will have to think and speak about negative circumstances. It was necessary for Paul and other early Church leaders to think about and address unpleasant and sensitive issues.

Thinking and speaking words of faith does not mean we live in a delusional bubble. We don't put our minds on hold; however, we operate according to our transformed mind, rather than our carnal mind (Romans 12:2).

Someone said, "Attitude determines altitude." To a great extent, our thoughts determine our destiny.

The more I think about God and the less I think about problems that I cannot change, the more peaceful I will be. The more I think about the Word, the more faith I will have. Abraham Lincoln is credited with saying, "I am what I think about all day long."

Do you prefer smiling to frowning? Think positive, faith-based thoughts.

We have the power to choose which direction we will take: Good or evil, positive or negative, life or death. Go ahead. Look at life from a positive point of view…through the lens of God's positive promises!

INTENTIONS

Some people use mind-altering drugs. How much better it is to use the mind-altering Word of God!

Hebrews 4:12 says, "For the word of God is quick, and powerful, and sharper than any twoedged sword, piercing even to the dividing asunder of soul and spirit, and of the joints and marrow, and is a discerner of the thoughts and intents of the heart."

Behind our thoughts are intentions. Thoughts and intentions are not the same. The two can be difficult to discern and separate. It is important that not only are our thoughts pure, but that the motives behind the thoughts are pure.

The Word of God is like a sharp sword that can divide between our thoughts and intentions. We must allow the Word of God to shine deep into our hearts and minds, deeper than any human being can see, deeper than even we usually look. We must be truthful and honest about our motives.

As we allow the Word of God to accurately identify our motives, we will find ourselves becoming more and more transparent and honest with God, with ourselves, and with others.

MIND CONTROL

You are like the air traffic control tower at an airport. You have the power to tell your thoughts what to do and where to go.

Some of Christians' biggest problems are due to their failure to control their thoughts. Instead of telling doubt, fear and negativity to move on, they let them land on the airstrip of their minds.

Negativity is rooted in fear and faithlessness. Michael Pritchard said it this way: "Fear is that little darkroom where negatives are developed."

II Timothy 1:7 says, "For God hath not given us the spirit of fear; but of power, and of love, and of a sound mind." A "sound mind" is a disciplined mind that we – through the power of the Word and Spirit of God – restrain and rule.

God has given us the power to control our thoughts. II Corinthians 10:3-5 tells believers, "For though we walk in the flesh, we do not war after the flesh: (For the weapons of our warfare are not carnal, but mighty through God to the pulling down of strong holds;) Casting down imaginations, and every high thing that exalteth itself against the knowledge of God, and bringing into captivity every thought to the obedience of Christ."

When your mind wants to take over, use spiritual weapons to defeat every unholy, ungodly, negative thought. The strong holds in your mind are no match for the mighty power of God. Instead of our minds holding us captive, we can hold them captive.

The things we allow our minds to think about are what will be reproduced in our speech and attitudes.

I Peter 1:13 says, "Wherefore gird up the loins of your mind." To gird means to tighten, to control, to put limits on. Since our words are a product of our thoughts, we need to "gird up" – strengthen, control – our minds.

I Peter 1:13 instructs us to take action, to *do* something. Our thoughts won't gird themselves.

Be proactive. Don't let your mind wander and dwell on whatever it wants to dwell on. Don't let your mind control you.

You – through the power of God and His Word – can control your mind.

CHAPTER 9

Straight Talk

WORDS THAT HURT

The childhood chant "Sticks and stones may break my bones but words will never hurt me" is a lie. Words can devastate children. Words can create within children a sense of worthlessness, defeatism, and hopelessness. Motivation to blossom and achieve can be crushed under the cruel hand of unkind, malicious words.

"You're stupid."

"You'll never amount to anything."

"Can't you do anything right?"

"I wish you'd never been born."

It is little wonder that many children turn to drugs at early ages. After all, drugs are painkillers. For a little while, at least, children can forget the pain of their lives. They can distract themselves from the words that have hurt them so deeply.

It is not just vulnerable children who are hurt by words. Adults can feel the sting too. To his friends who turned against him during the darkest hour of his life, Job – a husband and father – asked, "How long will ye vex my soul, and break me in pieces with words?" When Job needed encouragement and understanding, he instead felt the bitter lash of harsh, critical, accusatory words (Job 19:2).

We have all been hurt by the unkind and thoughtless words of others. We know how it feels to be deeply hurt by the things people say to us.

Regardless of how words have affected us, though, we should use our experiences to draw us into a closer relationship with Jesus. When we have been mistreated, we must take our hurt to the Lord and allow Him to pour in His healing balm and soothe us. Then we must pray for those who have hurt us in order to release ourselves from the bitterness in our hearts. These painful issues must be dealt with according to biblical principles of forgiveness (Matthew 5:43-45). Only then will the painful sting of hurtful words dissipate from our spirits.

The closer we get to Jesus, the more we will believe His Word instead of the hurtful words that have been said to us. When we realize how much Jesus loves us, it will matter less and less what others say to or about us. It won't matter that others have caused us to feel unloved and unwanted.

Jesus wants us. Jesus loves us.

MY WORDS

How have words spoken to you – good and bad – caused you to feel? How have they affected your life? How have they affected your relationships? How have unspoken words (i.e., the *absence* of positive, affirming words) influenced your life?

Since we know firsthand how powerful words are, we should be cautious and wise about our own choice of words. It makes sense that if we know how hurtful words can be that, if we want to be like Jesus, we take caution to not hurt people verbally.

Since we personally know how important it is to verbally affirm people and say kind things, we should look for opportunities to encourage people rather than discourage them.

If we want to please God, we must take responsibility for our own thoughts, words, and attitudes, regardless of what others do or say to us. We cannot control other people's choices, but with God's help, we can control our own actions and reactions.

We have all been hurt by people's words. However, it is much easier to talk and cry about how we've been hurt than it is to talk and cry about how we've hurt others. We tend to give ourselves a lot more grace than we give others.

We can apologize but we can never take back the words we speak. Though God's forgiveness covers sin, regardless of its nature, some actions are not restitutional. For example, God will forgive a murderer, but a murderer cannot restore life to the one he has murdered.

Since the tongue has the ability to destroy and we can never take back the words we speak, we need to carefully guard every word that we allow to come out of our mouths.

Say this: "*I* will take responsibility for *my* words. Regardless of what other people say, *my* words are *my* responsibility."

DEATH AND LIFE

The tongue is little, but it is an extremely influential part of the body. Proverbs 18:21 says, "Death and life are in the power of the tongue: and they that love it shall eat the fruit thereof."

Words have the power to destroy or build up.

Words have the ability to wound or heal.

Words can kill and words can give life.

Words can impart fear or faith.

Some people have only heard negativity all their lives, so speaking healing words is foreign to them. No matter how uncomfortable it may be for you to change your way of speaking, if you want to be an agent of life, you must alter your thoughts and speech.

Choose life. Choose to give life to others. In turn, you will discover that your entire demeanor and your relationships with others will benefit from your decision to choose life instead of death.

HEART TEST

In the previous chapter, we began to learn how to control our thoughts. Our thoughts produce words and actions. Matthew 12:34 says, "Out of the abundance of the heart the mouth speaketh."

Whatever is occupying the most space in your heart and mind is what will be reflected in your words. *People cannot see into our hearts but when we open our mouths they have an unobstructed view.*

Matthew 12:35 says, "A good man out of the good treasure of the heart bringeth forth good things: and an evil man out of the evil treasure bringeth forth evil things." Whatever is in your heart will come out of your mouth.

If you wonder if your heart is spiritually healthy or not, you can do a quick, simple test. You can gauge the condition of your heart by the words you speak.

If your words are unkind, rude, sarcastic, cynical, judgmental, critical, or demeaning, then your heart needs the attention of the Heart Surgeon. Your spiritual health is in grave danger.

If your words are kind, thoughtful, compassionate, honest, encouraging, gentle, uplifting, and sincere, then you have been taking measures to keep your heart healthy.

Is your treasure good or evil?

Is your heart healthy or sick?

TONGUE TAMER

James 3:7-8 says, "For every kind of beasts, and of birds, and of serpents, and of things in the sea, is tamed, and hath been tamed of mankind: But the tongue can no man tame; it is an unruly evil, full of deadly poison."

Here James presents us with a terrible predicament. He tells us that the tongue is an unruly evil, but that we cannot tame it. Humans can domesticate all kinds of wild animals. But the tongue, he says, is more unruly than any wild animal. This sounds like a problem with no answer.

But the answer is found in what seems to be the problem. Yes, no *man* can tame the tongue. But God can. We are powerless to tame our tongues by our own power. The method to taming the tongue lies in our reliance on the Holy Ghost to be active in our lives on a continual basis.

Perhaps one of the reasons God established speaking in another language to signify that a person has received the Holy Ghost is because when we submit our words to Him, the rest of us is submitted to Him also (Acts 2:4; 10:45-46; 19:6). James 3:2 says, "If any man offend not in word, the same is a perfect man, and able also to bridle the whole body."

The tongue is a little part of the body, but it is very powerful. James 3:5 says, "Behold, how great a matter a little fire kindleth!" He called the tongue "a fire, a world of iniquity" (3:6). The tongue is like a weapon of mass destruction. It is not very big but it packs a powerful punch.

David said that the tongues of his enemies were like sharp swords (Psalm 57:4; 64:3). In David's time, swords were weapons used in battle. They were created for the purpose of killing people. That is what David said the tongue is like.

As powerful and intimidating as our tongues are, they can be tamed by the Word of God and the Spirit of God. Ephesians 6:17 says that the Sword of the Spirit is the Word of God. The combination of the Word and Spirit of God is a joint weapon that the tongue cannot win against.

We activate the Word of God and the Spirit of God by prayer. It is not enough to have the Sword of the Spirit (Word of God) at our disposal. *Prayer is the way we submit to God, remove the Sword from its sheath and do battle against our tongues.* Without prayer, we will not succeed at controlling our tongues; rather, they will rule us.

Constant negativity and evil speaking are signs of a deeper, spiritual problem. If we attempt to change the way we think without relying on the Spirit of God to change us from the inside out, we will have nothing more than a carnal positive mental attitude. We might think we have it all together spiritually, but if we cannot bridle our tongues, James said that our efforts are vain (James 1:26). We must pray.

- Pray: "Let the words of my mouth, and the meditation of my heart, be acceptable in thy sight, O LORD, my strength, and my redeemer" (Psalm 19:14).

- Pray: "Lord, let my tongue be a subject of your Word and your Spirit. Let your Word and Spirit have all authority over my tongue today."
- Pray: "Set a watch, O LORD, before my mouth; keep the door of my lips" (Psalm 141:3).

When we surrender our tongues to God in prayer, we enable Him to control them when we cannot.

When we are tempted to verbally sin with our mouths, God will remind us of His Word that we have hid in our hearts to prevent us from sinning against Him (Psalm 119:11). The more Word there is in us, the more we will have to draw from in times of battle.

When we speak the Word, we are agreeing with God. Through prayer, Bible-reading, and meditation on the Word, God's thoughts and words gradually become our thoughts and words. As this happens, we will speak positive, pure, encouraging, and faith-building words.

Acts 4:13 says, "Now when they saw the boldness of Peter and John, and perceived that they were unlearned and ignorant men, they marvelled; and they took knowledge of them, that they had been with Jesus." Peter and John had spent time with Jesus and it showed in their actions and speech. They did not have ability on their own, but their communication with Jesus emboldened them to speak God's words.

As we submit our tongues to the Spirit and the Word of God and give Him authority over this most unruly member, His Spirit will tame our tongues. No, we cannot tame the tongue by our own ability, but God is an expert tongue tamer. Rely on Him to help you control your thoughts and words.

TIMING IS EVERYTHING

Ecclesiastes 3:7 says that there is "a time to keep silence, and a time to speak."

Proverbs 25:11 says, "A word fitly spoken is like apples of gold in pictures of silver."

Words properly placed in the right season are beautiful words, proper words, productive words.

The right words spoken at the right time can defuse difficult situations.

During Jesus' trial, He wisely chose when to speak and when to remain silent (Matthew 26:64; 27:11,14). He carefully considered which questions He would respond to. As He was being accused, He knew that, no matter what he said, His accusers would twist His words.

Isaiah 53:7 foretold Jesus' remarkable silence during His trial: "He was oppressed, and he was afflicted, yet he opened not his mouth: he is brought as a lamb to the slaughter, and as a sheep before her shearers is dumb, so he openeth not his mouth."

Sometimes the best response is to say nothing at all.

Proverbs 26:4-5 gives a seeming contradiction. "Answer not a fool according to his folly, lest thou also be like unto him. Answer a fool according to his folly, lest he be wise in his own conceit."

These back-to-back proverbs are not contradictory, though. They simply encourage the use of wisdom for dealing with different scenarios.

An example of this is found in the story of Nabal, Abigail, and David. I Samuel 25:3 describes Nabal as "churlish and evil in his doings." One of David's servants said of Nabal, "a man cannot speak to him" (I Samuel 25:17). In other words, Nabal could not be reasoned with.

David sent servants to ask Nabal to supply his army with provisions. Nabal was very wealthy but refused to help David. David was angry and made preparations to attack Nabal.

Without telling Nabal what she was doing, Abigail took food to David's men. By her wisdom, she prevented bloodshed. The next morning, she told Nabal what she had done. I Samuel 25:37 says that "his heart died within him, and he became as a stone." Ten days later, he died.

"Nabal" means "fool." Abigail understood that at times fools can be spoken to and other times it is best to keep silence around them.

Even if we have the answer people need, they are not always ready to receive it. Sometimes, speaking – even if we are speaking the truth – will create more problems than we want. We need to be sensitive to the Spirit and to the individual needs of people.

We need the wisdom of God to determine when to speak and when to keep silence. Wisdom is not just having the right words to say, but knowing when to say them. If we will live prayerful lives, the Lord will lead us and we will know when to speak and when to refrain from speaking.

WORDS: USE SPARINGLY

The wisdom of Proverbs 17:27-28 is priceless. "He that hath knowledge spareth his words: and a man of understanding is of an excellent spirit. Even a fool, when he holdeth his peace, is counted wise: and he that shutteth his lips is esteemed a man of understanding."

It has been said, "It is better to remain silent and be thought a fool than to open one's mouth and remove all doubt."

There is no shortage of talk in the world. Someone said, "Talk is cheap because supply exceeds demand." The vast majority of people are more than willing to offer their opinion anytime, anywhere.

But Ecclesiastes 5:2-3 says, "Be not rash with thy mouth, and let not thine heart be hasty to utter any thing before God: for God is in heaven, and thou upon earth: therefore let thy words be few. A fool's voice is known by multitude of words."

A person who does not chatter endlessly but chooses his words wisely will have more credibility than someone who talks nonstop about everything under the sun.

Proverbs 29:11 says, “A fool uttereth all his mind: but a wise man keepeth it in till afterwards.” Proverbs 10:19 says, “In the multitude of words there wanteth not sin: but he that refraineth his lips is wise.”

Proverbs 13:3 says, “He that keepeth his mouth keepeth his life: but he that openeth wide his lips shall have destruction.”

James admonished us to “be swift to hear, slow to speak” (James 1:19).

Talk less. Listen more.

LEARNING TO LISTEN

There is a dearth of good listeners in the world. Find a good listener and you have found a gem.

For many people, listening does not come naturally. Talking comes naturally, but becoming a good listener requires a lot of conscious effort. Most people don’t really hear what others are saying because, as another person is speaking, they are focused on formulating their response. Therefore, they are not fully listening.

Some people monopolize conversations. These people are usually talking about themselves and what they think and believe. Most of their sentences begin with "I."

I have known people who only wanted to talk incessantly about their problems and weigh everyone else down. They did not want a solution; they just wanted to talk.

People who constantly talk and rarely listen are probably motivated by a desire to be heard. Perhaps these people have suffered from a lifetime of rejection and think that by talking, they will receive some affirmation.

But dominating conversations is a selfish habit that backfires on the habitual talker. He or she ends up pushing people away instead of drawing them closer.

Do not dominate conversations and continually interrupt people. One-sided conversations do not build healthy relationships.

Good relationships are created when people can freely talk *and* listen. This is the basis of good communication.

Being a good listener does not mean that we have to completely agree with other people's thoughts and ideas. It means we care enough to allow them to express their thoughts and ideas.

A benefit of being a good listener is that we learn more by listening than we do by talking. When we talk, we generally only repeat what we already know. Listening enables us to learn something new. It gives us fresh perspective and new ideas.

God is the best example of a good listener. Every time we talk to Him, He listens. Follow His example and learn to show others that you care by listening to them.

TRASHCANS

While it is important that we need to be good listeners, we need to be selective about what and who we listen to.

"Sylvia, don't let anyone use your ears as a garbage can." This is some of the best and most useful advice my mother ever gave me. She only said it once and I was young, but it resonated with me then and has come to my rescue many times since.

My ears are not two little trashcans for people to dump whatever they want in, whenever they want. I don't have to allow people to drop their junk into my mind and spirit.

The things you allow into your mind via your eyes and ears should be clean and spiritually healthy. If you don't bring junk into your house, then you won't have to clean it out later.

Some people are more comfortable with spiritual clutter and filth than cleanliness and purity. It is normal for the world to gossip and talk about filthy things.

But the born again believer should resist being involved in ungodly conversation. Ephesians 5:12 says, "It is a shame even to speak of those things which are done of them in secret." We do not need to be educated about the debauchery and sin of the world and all the nuances of false doctrine in order to win people to Jesus. We don't need filthy, negative, and ungodly thoughts stockpiled in the storage rooms of our minds.

This is not head-in-the-sand thinking. We will hear more than we want to hear and learn more than we want to learn just by interacting with people day by day. We don't need to make a special effort to educate ourselves about all the intricacies of what worldly people are doing.

Images affect our thoughts. What we allow in our minds via our eyes and ears will affect our spirits, minds, hearts, thoughts, speech, and attitudes.

There are many reasons why I dislike television and why I carefully monitor what I look at online. Perhaps the biggest reason is because much of it is trash.

When we compare the vast majority of programming to the Bible, we find the two are diametric opposites. The Bible encourages us to live clean and pure lives. Hollywood encourages us to live filthy and polluted lives.

Why would I want to sift through a garbage dump to try to find something worthwhile? It is ridiculous to expect to be clean if I play in the trash pile all day.

When trash comes into your mind, whether it was dumped there by a person or the media, get it out as soon as possible. When we harbor ungodly words and images in our spirit, not only will we become discouraged, but we can also become cynical, disillusioned, faithless, cold in spirit, and bitter.

Protect your heart and spirit, eyes and ears. Keep your house clean!

DON'T BE A PARROT

The Bible refers to gossipers and slanderers as talebearers.

A talebearer's tongue always leaves destruction in its path. A talebearer is not an instrument of healing, but of pain. Proverbs 18:8 states, "The words of a talebearer are as wounds, and they go down into the innermost parts of the belly."

A talebearer makes bad situations worse.

"He that repeateth a matter separateth very friends" (Proverbs 17:9).

Distance yourself from talebearers and watch strife come to a grinding halt. "Where no wood is, there the fire goeth out: so where there is no talebearer, the strife ceaseth" (Proverbs 26:20).

A talebearer can't keep a secret. He thrives on spreading around bad news. Proverbs 11:13 says, "A talebearer revealeth secrets: but he that is of a faithful spirit concealeth the matter." A talebearer is not your friend. You cannot trust a talebearer.

Confidentiality is an admirable trait. From a young age I observed that some people can be trusted with secrets and others cannot. If I knew that someone habitually talked about other people and their problems, I mentally marked that person as untrustworthy. After all, if people openly and unashamedly talk about others, what would keep them from talking about me when I'm not around?

It is important that we carefully choose who we confide in. Talebearers are not worthy of our trust.

Talebearers are not usually content to just pass gossip along; they twist, distort and embellish it as they talk.

Some people thrive on repeating gossip and negative news. Just because we hear something negative and bad does not mean we need to repeat it.

As we travel, people often tell me things about their lives or other people. These things are not always uplifting and there is not usually much I can do about the situations.

Unless there is a specific reason I need to tell my husband about these things, I refrain from repeating what I hear. Why should I put them in his mind so he has to think about them too?

Fortunately, I do not have a great memory, so these types of things people tell me usually dissipate from my mind in a short amount of time. I can generally remember the topic of discussion, but not all the details.

Do not ally yourself with gossipers and talebearers. For your closest acquaintances, choose people who speak encouraging words, rather than gossip and negativity. Take a note from Proverbs 20:19. "He that goeth about as a talebearer revealeth secrets: therefore meddle not with him that flattereth with his lips."

Always keep in mind that everything you speak is subject to being repeated by someone else. Using a "just between us" attitude during your conversation does not guarantee that the person you are talking to won't use a "just between us" attitude when she in turn repeats that juicy gossip to someone else. If you repeat a matter, be prepared to suffer the consequences if your secret gossip is discovered.

Ecclesiastes 10:20 says, "Curse not the king, no not in thy thought; and curse not the rich in thy bedchamber: for a bird of the air shall carry the voice, and that which hath wings shall tell the matter."

If it would embarrass you for the person you are talking about to find out what you are saying about him or her, don't say it.

Better yet, if it would bother you if you knew *you* were the subject of someone else's gossip, don't gossip about others.

SHHHHH!

Sometimes the best thing to say is nothing, particularly if you can't think of something good to say. Someone said, "The kindest word in all the world is the unkind word, unsaid." Winston Churchill said, "By swallowing evil words unsaid, no one has ever harmed his stomach."

It is sometimes necessary to "bite our tongues" so that we do not retaliate with words we will later regret. As my friend Doris Jaynes says, "Good Christians have sore tongues."

When in doubt, shut your mouth. I have kept myself from a lot of jams by clamping my mouth shut and smiling sweetly. I have learned that it is not always necessary to say what I am thinking.

CHRONIC CRITICISM

Some people constantly look for someone or something to criticize. It is a miserable way to live, but that is their habit.

Critical people are experts at finding fault with others, but rarely themselves. They expect everyone to meet their code of approval, but few rarely do.

When people speak disparagingly of others, it reflects badly on them, but they don't usually realize this.

Criticism is only a symptom of a deeper problem. Envy, jealousy, insecurity, and pride are the root problems.

It is difficult to not notice other people's problems. But our first reaction should not be to criticize.

Just as we want others to be kind to us and give us some leeway when we make mistakes, so should we do to others. We have never walked in their shoes and they might be experiencing things we are unaware of.

Criticism is not the answer.

Galatians 6:1 tells us what to do. "Brethren, if a man be overtaken in a fault, ye which are spiritual, restore such an one in the spirit of meekness; considering thyself, lest thou also be tempted."

Instead of speaking critical words, speak kind words of hope and restoration.

OPEN YOUR MOUTH

We understand that we need to stop speaking the wrong words, but what do we say instead?

Even if we do not gossip or speak negatively, the devil wants to silence us from speaking words of faith and hope. He wants to intimidate us and convince us to keep our mouths shut when it comes to showing love, sharing the gospel, and speaking kind words.

For most of my life I have generally let other people do most of the talking during conversations. Even when I had something worthwhile to contribute, I would keep silent. One day, in prayer, the Lord took me to a simple Scripture.

Matthew 5:2 says of Jesus, "He opened his mouth, and taught them, saying…" That little statement stuck out to me as though flashing neon lights surrounded it.

God was trying to let me know that Jesus had wisdom but in order for people to benefit from it, he had to open His mouth. He could not keep silent and expect people to understand more about God. No, He had to open His mouth and talk.

People won't comprehend most of the Bible without instruction. This usually involves teaching. The great commission was to Go and Teach. In order to teach, we have to be confident in what we know about the Word and open our mouths. In order to teach, someone has to speak. People won't understand the gospel by osmosis. Someone has to speak the Word.

If God has given you correct, balanced understanding of the Scriptures, don't be afraid to open your mouth. Share what you know. Share your testimony.

When it comes to good stuff, open your mouth. When it comes to praising God, when it comes to encouraging others, and when it comes to helping others draw closer to Him, open your mouth!

I CAN'T

"I can't forgive him/her."

"I can't overcome this sin in my life."

"I can't change the way I think."

If you speak sentences like these that begin with "I can't," chances are good that you won't.

You won't forgive.

You won't overcome.

You won't change.

Often, "I can't" really means "I won't."

Replace your "I can't" statements with "I can."

The next time, "I can't" begins to come out of your mouth, replace it with Philippians 4:13. "I *can* do all things through Christ which strengtheneth me."

Sometimes God will stretch you almost to the point where you think you can't stretch anymore.

But He knows what He is doing. During the stretching process, He is strengthening you.

You can.

STRAIGHT TALK DOS AND DON'TS

- Do not be contentious (Proverbs 26:21).
- Do not lie (Ephesians 4:25).
- Speak the truth in love (Ephesians 4:15).
- Do not closely associate with people who do not believe, speak, and obey the Word of God (I Timothy 6:3-5).
- Do not engage in vain, unprofitable discussions (II Timothy 2:14,16; Titus 3:9).
- Do not use filthy, or even questionable, words (Colossians 3:8).
- Be an example of believers by the words you speak (I Timothy 4:12).
- Don't be a drip. "A continual dropping in a very rainy day and a contentious woman are alike" (Proverbs 27:15).
- Use constructive and instructive – not destructive – words.

- Do not say things you do not really mean. Be sincere.

- Speak honest, healing, edifying words instead of hurtful words. Examples: "I was wrong." "I'm sorry." "Please forgive me." "I will change this behavior."

- Think before you speak. Most of us have been guilty of "sticking our foot in our mouth." We say things that embarrass ourselves, hurt others, or make a conversation awkward. If we pause and think before we speak, we will have less regrets about the words that come out of our mouths.

- Be polite. Say "Please," "Thank you," and "You're welcome."

- Think Kingdom thoughts and speak Kingdom words. You are royalty.

- Bring glory to God with your words. No longer must we offer animal sacrifices but God loves to receive the "fruit of our lips" as we thank Him and praise Him (Psalm 51:15-17; Hosea 14:2; Hebrews 13:15). Turn your negative, faithless words into words of praise and thanksgiving to your great big, wonderful God!

A SOFT REPLY

Conflict in relationships is inevitable. When conflict comes and you are right, yet the other party will not bend, don't raise your voice to try to get your point across.

The reason we raise our voices is because we feel like a situation is out of our control. We want to be heard. We become fearful and we mistakenly think that by raising our voices, we can convince someone to listen to us.

Raising your voice and insisting that things go your way is counterproductive.

When we truly trust God, we know that He is in control. We don't think that we need to take control. We are secure in Him. We know that He will remedy the situation.

Even if we feel like we are in need of kind words ourselves, when we are secure in Jesus, we can dispense kind words to others instead. It is not wrong to want to have our needs met but we should not expect others to give us the security that only Jesus can give us. We build our security with God through prayer, transparency, and openness with Him.

People who engage in war greatly increase their chances of dying in a battle. If we say mean words, we will probably have mean things said back to us. Jesus said to Peter, "Put up again thy sword into his place: for all they that take the sword shall perish with the sword" (Matthew 26:52). If you use your tongue as a weapon against others, expect to be injured by the sharp words of others.

Don't engage in heated verbal conflicts. Let God fight your battles.

When we unleash a flood of words upon someone, we feel a release but we feel lousy later. Usually, our unguarded response makes things worse, not better.

Unfortunately, we often take out our anger, bitterness and dysfunction on those we love the most, not necessarily those who we are angry with.

People who have a healthy relationship with Jesus do not feel compelled to retaliate verbally; they know that God will defend and justify them if necessary. We do not have to try to convince people that we are right. We can let God speak on our behalf.

Sometimes we may be convinced that we are right, only to find out later that we are wrong. It pays to restrain ourselves from being too adamant and unyielding when there is even a slight possibility that we might be wrong. Someone said, "Keep your words soft and tender because tomorrow you may have to eat them."

Reply to anger with sincere tenderness. Do not respond to anger with anger. Control the tone and volume of your voice. Proverbs 15:1 says, "A soft answer turneth away wrath: but grievous words stir up anger."

If anger is stirred up, chances are good that harsh, hurtful words will escalate into even greater strife and division.

We should not allow our emotions to dictate to us. Angry replies will stir up strife, but soft replies will disarm and neutralize, paving the way for a resolution to conflict.

Keep in mind that someone has to be the first to reply softly. Take the initiative, pray as you speak, and respond with kindness and understanding. You can be the catalyst that can pave the way for good communication and strong relationships.

THE LAW OF KINDNESS

As important as the words we speak is the attitude in which they are carried.

Proverbs 31:26 says, "She openeth her mouth with wisdom; and in her tongue is the law of kindness."

In a nutshell, wisdom is living a well-ordered life. When we open our mouths, our words should be well ordered and filtered through the Word of God.

We should live according to the law of kindness. It should govern our words, especially when dealing with difficult people.

Ephesians 4:29-32 instructs, "Let no corrupt communication proceed out of your mouth, but that which is good to the use of edifying, that it may minister grace unto the hearers.

"And grieve not the holy Spirit of God,

whereby ye are sealed unto the day of redemption.

"Let all bitterness, and wrath, and anger, and clamour, and evil speaking, be put away from you, with all malice:

"And be ye kind one to another, tenderhearted, forgiving one another, even as God for Christ's sake hath forgiven you."

A BRIDLE FOR YOUR TONGUE

Psalm 39:1 says, "I will take heed to my ways, that I sin not with my tongue: I will keep my mouth with a bridle, while the wicked is before me."

It is important that we bridle our tongues, especially when we are around unbelievers.

The world abounds with cynicism, sarcasm, and pessimism. A lot of people are highly skilled at grumbling and complaining. It is not hard to find bad news. People hear enough negativity without hearing it from us too.

When I was first married, I worked at Burger King for about a year. It was certainly not a glamorous job, but a Bible college education does not equip a person with many marketable skills!

We needed the income, so I did the best job I could. When I took people's orders, I looked them in the eye, smiled and did my best to be cheerful.

One day, while working the drive-thru, a customer remarked, "You should be on a Burger King commercial. Are you on a Burger King commercial?"

I thought that was a funny question, but I realized that it was my smile and cheerfulness that motivated his compliment.

Non-believers will take note of someone who speaks positively, is happy, and smiles. There is little true joy in the world.

Ask yourself, "Based on my attitude, are people happier when I arrive or happier when I leave?" People should feel better by being around us, not worse.

Whatever is in a vessel is what will be poured out to others. What kind of words are you feeding your family, your co-workers, your friends and strangers?

A sour spirit appeals to no one. Except, maybe sour people like other sour people so they can be sour together. I'm not sure, but I do know that it is a whole lot nicer to be biblically positive than carnally negative.

When we are out-and-about, at the grocery store, at a restaurant, at the gas station, we should be friendly. In fact, we should be the kindest, most considerate people on the planet.

If you wake up so grouchy that you want to growl at everyone and everything, stay home and pray through. The postal clerk or gas station attendant does not need more negativity in his life, especially from someone who is a disciple of Jesus. Self-pity is not the way to share the light of the gospel. We all have bad days, but we should be careful to not take out our frustration and anger on people who don't even know God.

Relax.

Lighten up.

Enjoy your life.

Don't hide your light under a bushel.

Share your joy with your world.

LIFE ON A HIGHER PLANE

A lot of people engage in unspiritual prattle, words that fill the air but have little substance. Their words add little good to people's lives.

Some people talk themselves right into depression and negativity. This is a terribly inferior way to live. God has called us to a higher plane. We are new creations in Christ. We should not think and speak the same way we used to think and speak.

When we speak negative words, we have to listen to them too. They are infecting our spirit just as much or more than they are the person we are talking to. In reality, we are polluting ourselves with our own words!

Yuck. There is a much better way to live.

Even when we are around angry and negative people, we should not justify our unpleasant reactions by saying, "I'm only human. I'm just responding how humans respond."

God knows that we are only human but He also knows that He has empowered us with His Holy

Spirit. Our lives have been forever changed by the supernatural power of God.

Because of our new identity, we are able to live on a higher plane. As the Word guides our thoughts and words, we are able to not only withstand infection from the negativity around us, but we can be agents of change to help others learn to live on a higher plane also.

GET HONEST

I have never considered cursing an acceptable way to communicate.

But even though I have never been in the habit of cursing, there have been many times statements have come out of my mouth that I wished I could pop back in.

Psalm 139:4 says, "For there is not a word in my tongue, but, lo, O LORD, thou knowest it altogether."

Sometimes it is later, long after a conversation has ended, that God talks to me about something I said. It might not have even affected anyone, but God wants me to speak holy words, and He will convict me when my speech and attitude go even a tiny bit astray. He knows that I want to please Him and try to weed out of my life every remnant of carnality.

It doesn't matter who we are, we will all struggle with some aspect of "evil speaking," whether it is cursing, gossip, negativity, or telling outright lies.

I used to be rather cynical and sarcastic. Through the years, God has dealt with me about my cynicism and sarcasm. I came to realize that those attitudes are not pleasing to God and they do not bless the hearer.

Also, I can be a little too straightforward at times. This is a great approach with some people, but not all. For example, people who live in New England are very straightforward and appreciate frank speaking. But people in other parts of the United States are not as forthright.

I have shared with you aspects of my speech that I have identified in my life that needed to change. Now, it is your turn.

Ask yourself: "What aspects of my speech do I need to change? Do my conversational habits please God? How can I alter my speech patterns to bless others more?"

If we do not change our behavior (thoughts, mindsets, tone of voice, etc.), years from now we will still be treating people the same way. Life is too short to be unhappy, faithless, and negative.

How we speak is a choice, a habit, a learned behavior. When transitioning from negative thoughts and words to positive thoughts and words, it will "feel" awkward and the temptation to revert to the comfortable will be strong.

But once we make the shift, we will have developed a pattern, a habit of thinking godly thoughts. The change is worth the effort.

WORDS THAT HEAL

Words can hurt, but they can also heal.

Words can cause a confused teenager to receive hope for her future.

Words can comfort a lonely elderly widow.

Words can restore marriages.

Words can give a child security.

Words can cause employees to know that their employer values them.

Words can motivate a disabled individual to focus on what he can do, rather than what he can't do.

Words can tell drug addicts and alcoholics that there is more to life than their addictions and pain.

Words can encourage a tired mother and let her know that someone is noticing her hard work and sacrifice.

Yes, words can be agents of healing, restoration, and hope.

Proverbs 10:20 says "The tongue of the just is as choice silver."

Proverbs 15:26 says, "The words of the pure are pleasant words."

Proverbs 16:24 tells us that "Pleasant words are as an honeycomb, sweet to the soul, and health to the bones."

We all like pleasant words. Edifying words. Uplifting words. Encouraging words. Healing words. Kind words.

Let's speak them. We never know who might need them.

CHAPTER 10

My Enemy, My Friend

CONSTANT COMPANIONS

Every day, multiple times a day, we experience them in full force. They are with us everywhere we go. When we wake up, they are there. We take them to work with us. They go to the store, the park, and church. They are present at every conversation we have. When we read, when we study, when we play a game with our families, they are there.

When we have a disagreement with our boss, a family member, a person at church, they make themselves known.

When something good happens – we receive a gift, we get a promotion – they are there.

No matter what occurs in our lives – good, bad, or mundane – we simply cannot get away from them.

They are our emotions. And they influence you and your relationships more than you probably think. They also affect your health, for better or for worse.

DEFINING EMOTIONS

Emotions are defined as "a natural instinctive state of mind deriving from one's circumstances, mood, or relationships with others."[1]

Psychologists differentiate between emotions and feelings, saying that emotions react to stimuli, and feelings are the byproduct of emotions. I am not a psychologist, so I will use the terms interchangeably, since they are so similar and I think, in most people's minds, there is not much difference.

Some emotions, such as sadness, despair, confusion, and anxiety are perceived as negative. Other emotions, such as happiness, relief, pleasure, and hope, are perceived as positive. Depending on the circumstances, we might feel nervous, tense, disappointed, elated, excited, and confident all in the same day!

MY ENEMY, MY FRIEND

In and of themselves, most emotions are not bad. When we lose a loved one, when we are in a traumatic situation, even when something good occurs, emotions are God's way of allowing us to process and respond to what has happened to us.

Emotions can be a great gift. They can also be a great detriment.

For example, anger is an emotion. Psalm 7:11 reveals to us that "God is angry with the wicked every day." The Bible often refers to God's anger.

The Bible says it is okay to be angry – even God gets angry – but we should not allow our anger to control us and cause us to perhaps lash out at someone with our words and hurt them. Ephesians 4:26 says, "Be ye angry, and sin not: let not the sun go down upon your wrath."

It is okay to be angry. It is not okay to allow our anger to turn into sin.

Emotions are natural and acceptable to God. After all, He is the one who created us with emotions. But He does not approve of uncontrolled negative emotions that cause us to sin. In His Word, God gives us specific instructions about how to deal with different emotions.

During times of stress, we tend to put our minds on hold. We cannot trust our emotions. We must learn to rely on the Word of God.

EMOTIONS VERSUS REALITY

If we allow them free reign, our emotions can distort reality. Circumstances and people can seem much worse or better than they actually are.

We can't always rely on our emotions. Our emotions can lie to us. They can deceive us.

We must separate our emotions from reality.

People tend to believe, "Whatever I think/believe/feel is true." They put a lot more stock in what they think/believe/feel than they do in what is actually true.

Here are some examples of feelings that can masquerade as reality if we allow them to:

- *"I feel like my husband will never change."*
- *"I feel like this sickness is going to kill me."*
- *"I feel like nobody at church likes me."*
- *"I feel like something bad is about to happen."*

Sometimes we think/believe/feel things that have no validity. We make them reality only in our minds. We *feel* things about the future that are completely groundless because we allow our minds to dwell on negativity and darkness, rather than the power of God in our lives.

The Word of God is reality, not our feelings. We must learn to believe and obey the Word and apply it to our lives. The Word of God will bring a balance to our emotions.

- *I feel insecure.*

This feeling results in depression, passive-aggressive behavior, or blatant control issues. The root of insecurity is fear.

"I will say of the LORD, He is my refuge and my fortress: my God; in him will I trust" (Psalm 91:2).

Instead of giving in to feelings of insecurity, trust in God! Only He can give you the security you want and need.

- *I feel inferior.*

This feeling results in negative behavior and negative words ("I can't achieve anything." "I am so dumb.")

Or, it results in an arrogant approach used to try to cover up the feelings of inferiority, in an attempt to divert the attention away from the real problem. ("I am the best." "It's all about me.")

Philippians 4:13 says, "I can do all things through Christ which strengtheneth me." This verse silences the "I feel inferior" voice.

"I can do all things…" There is not a "maybe" before the "I can." What is more positive than that?

"…through Christ which strengtheneth me." There is the secret. Everything good we accomplish will be "through Christ." He is the one who will strengthen and enable us as we lean upon His strength and power.

The "I feel inferior" line and others like it focus on self. Believing "I can do all things through Christ which strengtheneth me" puts the attention back on God, where it belongs.

When we are God-centered instead of self-centered, the feelings of inferiority will vanish because we will be focused on His power, goodness, and love rather than our own weaknesses, pasts, and inabilities.

- *I feel fearful.*

Fear is an instinctual response, a defense mechanism that motivates us to protect ourselves. For example, if you heard a burglar breaking into your house, fear would motivate you to act. Fear catapults you to defend yourself if you are about to be hit by a car or if a big bear in the woods is headed your way.

But most of the time our fears are based upon our past experiences, mostly related to emotional pain incurred by people in our pasts. This type of fear can be debilitating. It can cause people to think and act irrationally and inhibit the health of their current relationships, all because they expect their painful pasts to replicate themselves in present relationships. Fear sets in and they sabotage relationships through things like jealousy. They try to control people and circumstances. Many times, desire to control stems from insecurity, pain, hurt, a life that has been vandalized. They do not live by the Word of God, but by the fear that they allow to captivate them.

Fear is more than an emotion; it is a spirit. "For God hath not given us the spirit of fear; but of power, and of love, and of a sound mind" (II Timothy 1:7). In the chapter "Fear's Worst Nightmare," we learned that if we are fearful, it is not the Spirit of God that gave us the fear. Instead of fear, God gives people wonderful things like power, love and a sound mind! "There is no fear in love; but perfect love casteth out fear: because fear hath torment" (I John 4:18).

- *I feel lonely.*

This feeling is often accompanied by feelings of isolation and abandonment. If you have received the Holy Ghost, you are never alone! Hebrews 13:5-6 tells us, "I will never leave thee, nor forsake thee. So that we may boldly say, The Lord is my helper, and I will not fear what man shall do unto me."

You don't have to pretend that everything in your life is wonderful. In fact, people who are emotionally healthy can honestly acknowledge what is bothering them without allowing it to control their lives.

But we must constantly go back to what the Word says. The Word – not our emotions – should be the final authority in all matters.

EMOTIONAL HIGHS

It is rarely a good idea to make emotion-based decisions. It has been said, "When emotion is high, judgment is low."

This is why people whose spouses die are sometimes advised to not make any major decisions for a year. They need time to be able to think things through, instead of acting rashly as a result of their grief.

Even good emotions, if they are unusually high, can alter judgment. Many young couples, intoxicated by emotion, get married only to discover that they made their decision based on emotion alone, without contemplating the commitment required to make a long-term relationship successful. Their decision to marry is sometimes made prematurely because they define love through the lens of their emotions. They don't realize that true love is not simply an emotion, but a commitment.

When we allow our emotions to control us, we become self-focused and prideful. The focus turns from God to us. That is why it is so easy for us to sin and do irrational things when we allow our emotions to dictate our actions. Whether our emotions are high as a result of something good or low as a result of something bad, we must try to remember that judgment can be clouded at such times.

If you don't think you can make good judgment calls about your life because of your out-of-control emotions, ask your pastor or a truly spiritual and prayerful friend for help. It is times like these that we need to tap the resources in the body of Christ for support and spiritual guidance and wisdom.

FRUIT VERSUS FEELINGS

The fruit of the Spirit – love, joy, peace, longsuffering, gentleness, goodness, faith, meekness, and temperance – help us navigate our way through life. When they are active in our lives, they keep us from being manipulated by events and circumstances. We will be less likely to allow our emotions to dictate to us.

But the fruit of the Spirit are not feelings. They are fruit. For example, I can love someone even when I don't *feel* love toward them. I can have peace when I am hurt and grieving. I can be gentle even when my feelings want me to be vengeful. I can have faith when I feel frustrated.

When the fruit of the Spirit are active in our lives, the works of the flesh, which are nemesis to the fruit of the Spirit, have less power over us (Galatians 5:19-23). We are less likely to allow our fleshly nature or our feelings to tell us what to do.

FAITH VERSUS FEELINGS

Faith is not an emotion.

If we find ourselves trying to work up enough emotion so we will "feel" faith, we are barking up the wrong tree. Faith is both a fruit of the Spirit and a gift of the Spirit, but it is not an emotion.

We cannot work up enough emotion to produce miracles. Miracles are supernatural products of a supernatural force: Faith. "I *feel* healed" or "I don't *feel* healed" has nothing to do with healing. Healing is divine in origin and not dependant on what we feel.

When we obey the Word and are prayed for, we simply – by faith in the Word of God and our obedience to it – accept that God has answered the prayer. That is what He said He would do and He never lies.

Whether or not we *feel* healed has nothing to do with faith. Results do not precede faith; faith precedes results. We do our job (believe) and let God do His job (heal).

BEYOND FEELINGS

I have a passport that says I am a citizen of the United States of America. It does not matter whether or not I feel American. The truth is that I am an American.

Gideon did not feel very powerful but God called him a "mighty man of valour" (Judges 6:12). What God says is the reality, the fact, the truth…not what we feel.

We might feel inadequate to do what God calls us to do. We might feel drained and tired. Yet, if we are relying on God's strength and power, He will always come through regardless of how we feel.

Beyond our feelings of insufficiency, incompetency, and helplessness is the great power of God. Often, it is when we acknowledge our limitations that His greatness shines the brightest!

"I FEEL…"

In 2011, when we were working as AIMers in Israel, we went to Jerusalem's Old City with James and Charlotte Wholters, friends of ours, and their three children. We were looking for St. Mark's Church, one of the locations identified as the possible site of the Upper Room.

I was leading the way, since the Wholters had never been to St. Mark's Church. We walked up and down cobblestone steps and through the narrow alleyways of the Old City. As we rounded a turn, I stopped, thinking, trying to orient myself to my surroundings.

Almost to myself, I said, "I feel like we are really close to it."

Instantly, James started laughing. "Feel!" he exclaimed.

Then, jesting, he said to Bill, "I *feel* like we are really close to it."

He continued to jokingly mimic me for a few minutes.

James is a military guy and I doubt if he places a high priority on surface emotions and feelings. It was funny, even though I was the one being made fun of. But it was also an illustration of the difference between men and women.

Think about this. How often do you hear women say, "I feel…?"

A lot! We women use that term on a regular basis. In fact, "I feel" is so much a part of our vocabulary that we probably don't even realize how frequently we say it.

But how often do you hear a guy say, "I feel…?"

Probably not very often, unless he is talking about something tangible, as in, "I feel the pain in my broken leg." Yeah.

MAN-BRAIN VERSUS WOMAN-BRAIN

While a few men are highly emotional and some women are very analytical, most women are more emotionally wired than men.

Women are much more in tune with people who are hurting emotionally. And most men are ready to offer a solution. They pull out their toolbox and are ready to fix everything.

But women will listen. They will cry when someone else is crying. The human-interest aspects of world poverty, tornadoes that tear people's homes apart, and war refugees, easily move them. Men tend to look at things more objectively.

From a woman's vantage point, men are unfeeling, harsh, insensitive, and cold. But, usually, they are none of those things. They are just using the man-brain God gave them. We want them to be openly tender and sensitive and talk a lot about their feelings. Actually, what we want is for them to be just like us and have a woman-brain!

God made us women with women-brains and they fit well in our God-appointed profession of motherhood because women make excellent mothers. We mother better than men because we are natural nurturers. We care about all the little details of our children's lives and that is what makes us good mothers.

Men, on the other hand, would not make good mothers. But – with their reasoning skills and long-range sight – they make great fathers.

Our emotions can be a great blessing, the perfect counterpart to our more rational husbands. Because we care so deeply for people and have a lot of compassion, we have a great capacity to minister, especially through intercessory prayer.

But if we allow them to, our emotions can overwhelm us personally.

One of our greatest strengths can also be one of our greatest detriments. It is important that we allow our husbands to be men and help balance us.

"Let's look at empathy. There are three kinds: *cognitive* empathy, being able to know how the other person sees things; *emotional* empathy, feeling what the other person feels; and empathic *concern,* or sympathy – being ready to help someone in need.

"Women tend to be better at emotional empathy than men, in general. This kind of empathy fosters rapport and chemistry. People who excel in emotional empathy make good counselors, teachers, and group leaders because of this ability to sense in the moment how others are reacting.

"Here's where women differ from men. If the other person is upset, or the emotions are disturbing, women's brains tend to stay with those feelings. But men's brains do something else: they sense the feelings for a moment, then tune out of the emotions and switch to other brain areas that try to solve the problem that's creating the disturbance.

"Thus women's complaint that men are tuned out emotionally, and men's that women are too emotional – it's a brain difference.

"Neither is better – both have advantages. The male tune-out works well when there's a need to insulate yourself against distress so you can stay calm while others around you are falling apart – and focus on finding a solution to an urgent problem. And the female tendency to stay tuned in helps enormously to nurture and support others in emotional trying circumstances. It's part of the 'tend-and-befriend' response to stress."[2]

Because they have a man-brain, not a woman-brain, men are not fully equipped to know how to deal with women's shifting emotions. Show them your broken leg or the scratch on your arm and they're okay; they can deal with that. They can *do* something, such as take you to the hospital.

But where are these nebulous feelings we talk so much about? Men can't see them or touch them. So they can't fix them or come up with a solution. And that gives them anxiety!

Men have to *learn* to listen to women express their emotions. Listening to women express their emotions does not come natural to guys because they do not understand our emotions. They have to learn that it is important that they simply care enough to listen to us express what we are thinking and feeling, even if they can't fix everything.

As they allow the Spirit of God to work in their lives, they will find themselves becoming better listeners, more sensitive, more compassionate, and more caring.

But expecting men to completely understand us is unreasonable. Remember, no matter how willing your husband is to allow God to help him love you better, he still has a man-brain!

Accept your husband for who he is. Communicate with him as best as you can, but realize his ability to understand you is limited by his man-brain.

Don't forget God; He understands you better than anyone else; in fact, He understands you better than you understand yourself! He is the One who created you with emotions. He is the perfect listener and perfect friend.

Appreciate your husband's strengths and let God take up any slack in your emotional life.

DEBUNKING MYTHS

- *"I have no control over my emotions."*

This person is like a runaway train. You never know what destruction she will create. She is an emotional marshmallow and her life is like a nonstop roller coaster.

With the help of God, master your emotions before they master you!

- *"Emotions are who I am, an extension of my self. I must always express them."*

Emotions are a part of us, and it is sometimes healing to express them, but they are *not* the sum total of who we are.

- *"Love is a feeling."*

Love is much, much, much more than just a feeling. Some people are more committed to loving the idea of being in love than they are to actually loving someone. Whether or not I feel love towards someone is not the primary determining factor of whether I actually love him or not.

Many successful marriages go through testing periods, when one or both spouses do not feel like he or she loves the other. As they persevere, even when the feelings of love wane, in the long run, their marriage becomes stronger than ever before. It becomes predicated less upon emotions and more upon commitment.

EMOTIONAL DISORDERS

These days, there is a plethora of labels for a wide range of mental and emotional disorders, from anxiety disorders to eating disorders. We knew a family with a three-year-old who could rattle off her labels the way some kids talk about their collections of toys.

Labels infer that we are helpless to change our emotional condition.

Uncontrolled emotions can affect our physical health. They can weaken our immune systems, give us high blood pressure, stomach ulcers, and headaches. They can also create an imbalance in our minds.

Americans seem to be addicted to psychiatric solutions because they have rejected God as their answer. Pharmaceutical drugs, therapy, psychology, and counseling might help somewhat in extreme cases, but these methods will never completely heal a person of mental and emotional disorders. Often, rather than fix the real problems, these methods only mask them.

I do not pretend to be qualified to remark further on this potentially controversial topic, but I do believe in the power of our God to help anyone out of any problem. My primary message in this section is to simply encourage anyone who bears the label of an emotional disorder to realize that God has empowered you to change. If you will not accept a label, if you will put forth some effort to change, God will help you.

Emotional health requires us to confront *ourselves*, not everyone else. We don't expect everyone else to behave perfectly before we have peace, contentment and rest. We don't attempt to change anyone except ourselves, and we admit that we can only change with the help of God.

THREE DIMENSIONS

Jesus said, "And thou shalt love the Lord thy God with all thy heart, and with all thy soul, and with all thy mind, and with all thy strength: this is the first commandment" (Mark 12:30).

We could call this comprehensive love. God wants us to love Him with every component of our being. Included are our emotions, which are an inherent part of who we are. If God wants us to love Him with our emotions, how do we best do that?

I believe there are three dimensions we enter as we learn to love God with our emotions. Often, the three dimensions overlap. Our ultimate goal should be to live in the third dimension.

DIMENSION ONE: EMOTIONAL RELEASE

All of my life, I have seen people come to church distraught and emotionally troubled. As others begin to praise God, these people find it easy to pray as God draws them. He begins to deal with them about their lives and perhaps painful things they are going through. Often, as they begin to feel the presence of God, they cry. Tears in the presence of God give them a temporary relief from pain. So they feel a release from the emotional and mental tension. For a while, they *feel* better.

Yet, some do not make any commitments to God. They do not make any lasting, permanent changes. *They do not let God deal with the root issues in their lives.* They do not enter into the presence of God far enough for Him to begin to give them the security and comfort they so desperately need. They get only far enough to release a little emotion and they *feel* better. After all, who doesn't feel better after a good cry, surrounded by the presence of God and people who love you?

As a result, they leave feeling lighter but nothing has really changed. Soon, life will draw them back into the same whirlpool of busyness and stress that they were in before. They *feel* better for a little while but they are not *actually* better.

We can become obsessed with feeling emotional when we pray. If we can't drum up enough emotion, we don't *feel* like we have prayed. Wrong. Where in the Bible does prayer require emotion? Yes, we often get emotional when we pray, but prayer is simply communication with God. So if we talk to God, we have prayed, whether we were emotional or not.

We need to discern the difference between just receiving a temporary emotional release and making permanent changes.

DIMENSION TWO: FEELING GOD'S PRESENCE

Usually, when we have been deeply hurt, when we are disappointed, or when we have experienced a loss, we have emotions that are out of control. But the root is even deeper than our emotions. The root is in our heart and our spirit. Only God can heal something that deep. And He can only heal us when we enter deep into His presence and become transparent before Him.

The change we need won't come through a momentary emotional release. An emotional release alone is not a replacement for spending time in the presence of God.

Our change won't come through human will power.

It won't come just by changing our minds and the way we think.

It won't come by barreling through life, suppressing our emotions and pretending everything is fine. Suppressing our emotions, thoughts, and feelings to the point of not taking action to overcome is a counterproductive way of dealing with life.

Wholeness only comes when we allow the Spirit and Word of God to work together to heal what has been broken in our lives. And it is only when our spirits become broken before Him in His presence, acknowledging how much we need His help that He can pour in His healing balm.

This is where we pray past the point of an emotional release and allow God to minister, not just to our emotions, but those hidden rooms of our hearts that we have kept quarantined for so long because we fear being hurt if we are too transparent.

The safest place in the world is in the presence of the Lord. It is a place where we can pour out our hearts to God, be vulnerable, yet assured that God will never hurt us. As God ministers to you, you will find your fear vanishing and you will become more transparent around others also.

God wants to help us, but often we do not linger long enough in His presence for Him to really minister to us the way we need to be ministered to. We are restless, eager to move on to what is comfortable. We don't want God touching the painful areas of our lives.

We should learn to pray past the point of an emotional release. God understands our need for an emotional release and He wants to ease our burdens. And there is no better place to go for an emotional release than the presence of God.

But God wants us to learn to stay in His presence. When our emotions have calmed, we should linger and listen for His voice. He might want to talk to us about something in our lives that needs to change. He might want to give us direction about a situation. He might just want to spend time with us because He loves us and wants to develop a deeper relationship.

Feeling God's presence is a priceless gift. Learn to enjoy His presence, to linger as He ministers to you with His love, gives you security, and gently washes over you with His incomparable peace.

In time, you will find yourself wanting to enter into the presence of God on a regular basis, not just when you need an emotional release from the stress of life. You can become addicted to being in the presence of God. It is satisfying, yet makes you want to return again and again. This is the best kind of addiction!

DIMENSION THREE: RELATIONSHIP DEVELOPMENT

I am glad that I can worship God with my emotions. I am glad that I do not have to suppress my emotions because of religious convention, as is the case in many churches, but am free to express my heartfelt gratitude to God for all He has done for me.

Many people have never felt the presence of God and I can think of few things sadder. Feeling God's presence is soothing, comforting, and energizing. He fulfills the deepest longing of human beings. When I feel His presence, I am completely content.

Worshipping and praising God with our emotions is biblical. God wants us to love Him with all of our heart, soul, mind and strength. We demonstrate our love for God through heartfelt praise and worship. Every component of our being – including our emotions – should get involved in praising God.

I think it is almost impossible for a person to pray sincerely without some emotion naturally coming to the surface. Our prayers are not rote and robotic. We don't pray our prayers from a book written by someone else. They come from our hearts. We have a very real relationship with God and our deep feelings for Him surface when we pray.

Many churches are using slogans such as "A place to belong" or "A place to connect." And it is true that the Church is a place to belong and connect.

People want to be loved. They have been emotionally damaged by hurtful relationships. Because of the pain in people's hearts, contemporary Christian songs, which focus on feeling the Spirit of God, resonate with them and draw them into God's presence. This is good. Psalm 62:8 is a beautiful invitation from the Lord: "Trust in him at all times; ye people, pour out your heart before him: God is a refuge for us."

However, focus on feeling the Spirit of God without also emphasizing the power of the Word of God and Scriptural truths, as older songs did, can create a vacuum and a false understanding of what living for God is all about.

Again, I do not need to feel God to pray, although I usually do feel Him during times of prayer.

I do not need to feel God to hear His voice.

The Bible speaks more of worship, praise, prayer, seeking the Lord, and obeying the Lord than it does of just feeling God. I praise Him just because He is worthy of praise and almost every time I benefit greatly by being able to feel His presence.

Although feeling the Spirit of God is awesome, our purpose in prayer should not be to just feel God. It should be to seek the Lord, draw close to Him, and hear His voice. It should be a time of renewal and cleansing.

Usually, somewhere during that process we will feel Him. But praying whether we feel Him or not indicates that we are maturing spiritually.

Paul wrote to Timothy, "I know whom I have believed, and am persuaded that he is able to keep that which I have committed unto him against that day" (II Timothy 1:12).

Paul suffered much for the gospel's sake. What he *knew* – not his emotions – sustained him.

In the midst of Job's trial, he *felt* estranged from God. He said, "Behold, I go forward, but he is not there; and backward, but I cannot perceive him: On the left hand, where he doth work, but I cannot behold him: he hideth himself on the right hand, that I cannot see him" (Job 23:8-9).

Job did not stop there, however. He said, "But he knoweth the way that I take: when he hath tried me, I shall come forth as gold" (Job 23:10). Job took comfort in what he *knew* about God.

The Word of God is powerful enough to sustain us regardless of the darkness of life and the unreliability of our emotions.

So, beyond an emotional release, even beyond feeling the presence of God, is a deep relationship with God where He speaks to us and ministers to us through His Word and His Spirit.

Life with God is a progressive journey. As we move forward, our relationship with Him grows stronger and, in time, we learn to rely less on our emotions and more on our obedience to the Word and Spirit of God.

THE PERFECT BALANCE

Here are some ideas for things to pray as you ask God for help with your emotions.

- "God you are greater than my emotions. You can bring a balance to my emotions. My emotions are closely tied to my thoughts, so help me to control my thoughts. Help me to think upon and apply Philippians 4:8 and other Scriptures that teach me how to gird up the loins of my mind."
- "Help me to allow you to be to me in my life all that I have lost and make up for all the hurt I have experienced. Help me to take everything to you in prayer and allow your Spirit to cleanse me and reassure me. Help me to accept the security and love that you want to give me."
- "God, help me to not react emotionally but to use your Word as a guide for my actions, words, and thoughts. Help me to make your Word a reality in my life, not just ink on paper."
- "God, certain times of the month can be especially difficult for me and cause me to be unpredictably moody. Help my hormones to not dictate my emotions. During these times, help me to be especially aware of the power

> my emotions can have over me and not allow them to rule my life."

When our emotions fail us, God's Word will still be strong enough for us to stand on. Many of the verses in Proverbs are rules for controlling our emotions. Combine prayer with reading the Bible. Personalize the Word by praying Scripture. Here is one to get you started that you might remember from the chapter "Stress Solutions":

"Hear my cry, O God; attend unto my prayer. From the end of the earth will I cry unto thee, when my heart is overwhelmed: lead me to the rock that is higher than I" (Psalm 61:1-2).

As you pray specifically and allow the Word to work in your life, you will notice that your emotions have less control over you. You will be able to direct your emotions properly and use them for good instead of bad. They will become less of an enemy and more of a friend!

CHAPTER 11

Person to Person

A NICE PLACE

Someone said, "The world would be a nice place if it were not for the people." Unfortunately, that statement contains a great deal of truth, considering that most of our problems in life involve people.

Because of relationship issues, some people become reclusive and cynical.

But if we change our mindset about person-to-person relationships, we will think of the world as a nice place, people and all.

Some of the principles we need to learn are difficult to accept, but in the long run they will help our relationships become more fulfilling than ever before.

HUMAN BEINGS

We want to believe that another person – whether it is Mom or Dad, Husband or Wife, Aunt or Uncle – will never hurt us. We want to believe in perfect people that we can always rely on and trust every moment of every day.

But such thinking is a huge setup for disappointment.

We can never 100% trust human beings. 99.99%, perhaps, but not 100%. Why not? Because they are human beings!

It is unrealistic to expect another person, no matter how wonderful and good they may be, to *never* let us down at some point in time. To place such an expectation on a person is to exalt them beyond the status of a human being.

The Bible is not a book about perfect people; it is a book about a perfect God. Allow the people in your life to be human. Appreciate those who are good and kind, but don't put them in the place of our infallible God.

Instead of being upset that people can't be everything to you, be thrilled that God can. Let humans be humans and let God be God.

If you can grasp this simple concept, it will liberate you and allow you to have more fulfilling relationships.

GOD FIRST

Along a similar train of thought, in your mind, disassociate God from every other relationship in your life. This sounds odd, so let me explain.

Many of us view God through the lens of our past relationships. If your father was harsh…or abusive…or absent from your life entirely, then you might tend to think of God in the same way. If your grandfather was demeaning and condescending, and his treatment causes you to live cowed down and viewing yourself as an inferior person, you might think that God views you the same way.

When people come to God, they tend to associate Him with how they have been treated in the past. They have not yet had time to cultivate their relationship with Him. They do not know enough of the Word to learn how deep and wide God's love is for them. All they have to gauge Him by is their past relationships.

God is not your earthly father. He is not your earthly mother, grandfather, grandmother, son, or daughter. He is not your earthly friend, boss, or neighbor.

In your mind, disconnect God from all of your past and present human relationships. We need to allow God to have His own identity and stop associating Him with people in our lives.

Even if you have had wonderful, healthy, fulfilling relationships in your life, you still need to keep God in His own category. He is God. Let people be people and let God be God.

We should not expect people to supply what only our God can give us: True, flawless, completely unconditional love and unfailing commitment.

This concept is not intended to demean any human relationship we have. Rather, it keeps God first. *When our foundation is built on God, all other good relationships add to our already complete lives in Christ (Colossians 2:10). Regardless of the ups and downs of our relationships, we will be stable.* Our relationship with God should be the most important relationship in our lives.

DON'T TRY TO CHANGE PEOPLE

A guaranteed way to be miserable is to try to change another person. We cannot change anyone. Even God cannot change people without their cooperation. He will work with them, trying to reach them with His love and truth, but if they don't want to change, He will not force them to.

It is not your job to fix people. You are not responsible for repairing other people's lives. You are not responsible for anyone else's level of peace and joy. Allow others to make their own choices. You cannot change anyone except yourself, and that only with God's help.

Don't wait for other people to change their behavior before you change yours. Their behavior is their responsibility and your behavior is your responsibility.

CHANGE YOURSELF

It is much easier to point out other people's faults than it is to look inward. But while we wait for other people to change, God waits for us to change.

Some people erroneously think they should be excluded from change. They think, *Everyone is worse than me so they should change, not me. I have a right to say what I want and behave how I want. This is how I have behaved for years and I'm not about to change now.*

We should not adopt that mindset. It will hinder our spiritual growth.

Whenever we have conflicts with people, we need to examine ourselves and see what about us, our behavior, attitudes, and speech needs to change. It is liberating to turn our focus away from people's problems and let God place His magnifying glass on our lives instead.

The older I get, the more inclined I am to pray, "Lord, help me learn something through this trial. Develop me. Show me *my* flaws."

The things about us that need to change can only be revealed as we are able to handle the revelations. The more transparent we are before God, the more of our lives He fine-tunes. And that draws us closer to Him because there are fewer obstructions between Him and us.

What a win-win situation!

WHAT TO DO WHEN THEY DON'T

The cold, hard truth is that some people never do change. Or, they change very, very slowly. We have no way of knowing who will change and serve God and who will not.

This sounds pessimistic, but there are many biblical examples of people who refused to change. Their refusal tied God's hands to work in their lives. Esau and Saul are examples.

This sad fact presents us with a dilemma. Will we continue to try to change people or will we trust God with their lives?

Our best course of action is to keep our focus on Jesus. Regardless of what others do or don't do, if we lose our focus on Jesus, we will find ourselves spiraling downward spiritually. We will become discouraged because of other people's actions.

There is a song that says, "Turn your eyes upon Jesus. Look full in His wonderful face. And the things of this world will grow strangely dim in the light of His glory and grace." It is a beautiful song full of promise. Notice that the song does *not* say, "Turn your eyes upon *people*." That would be a formula for disaster!

Pray for people who don't seem to want to change their ways. God knows how to talk to them in ways they can understand. When you pray, don't pray with the motive of wanting to make people exactly like you. Ask the Lord to help them develop into the person that *He* wants them to be.

Unfortunately, your life might become uncomfortable and even painful at times because of other people's stubbornness and pride, but if you will stay focused on Jesus, He will give you strength and grace that you never had before. Instead of resenting them, you will find yourself developing patience and kindness toward the people in your life who are struggling.

If you will stay focused on Jesus, His Spirit will fill in the cracks of your life that have developed because of unfulfilling relationships.

TIPS FOR HEALTHY RELATIONSHIPS

In addition to the principles already presented in this book such as becoming a good listener, expressing appreciation, and speaking uplifting words, here are some tips that you can apply to any relationship in your life that you want to improve.

- *Be kind.*

This sounds simple, but sometimes it is hard to do.

Even if people are not kind to you, be kind to them. How else will they learn how to be kind unless they watch someone else doing it?

The importance of being kind cannot be overstated.

- *Do something nice.*

Our society tends to be rather self-centered. Part of healthy relationship building is doing what will please someone else, instead of "seeking our own" all the time.

Do nice things for people without expecting anything in return, even a "Thank you." Make his favorite meal. Give a compliment. Smile. Babysit once in a while.

Little things can make a big difference.

- *Give people the benefit of the doubt.*

Many communication problems are the result of expecting people to think and behave exactly how we think and behave. When someone is harsh, standoffish, or hateful, there is always a reason for it and often it has nothing to do with you. People usually react because of past hurt that has never been healed. You don't know what they might be going through.

If you are hurt by someone's words and actions, don't harbor the hurt in your heart. Pray blessings upon their lives and, if they will allow it, reach out to them with love and kindness.

- *Pray first.*

Most people do not like confrontation. However, to build healthy relationships, confrontation is sometimes necessary.

If you have to confront someone about a sensitive issue, pray before you communicate with him or her. Ask the Lord to help you approach the situation with the right spirit. Prayer allows God to reveal to us our true motives.

If you will communicate with God before you communicate with people, He will guide you with wisdom and give you a calm demeanor even if the topic is sensitive and emotionally charged.

- *Be honest about your own flaws.*

Depending on how we were raised, this may be easier for some people than others. Generally speaking, though, I think it would be safe to say that none of us like to admit our faults, even when they are staring us in the face.

But no human being is perfect and if we act like we are, the only ones we are fooling is ourselves. Nobody is right about everything all the time.

Some people would not admit a flaw – even a little one – if you paid them. Anybody can say, "Nobody's perfect" or "We all have our faults." Those are really good copouts.

Honest people admit their own flaws. If they wrong someone, they are willing to confess their faults (James 5:16).

If someone points out your flaws and offers advice and correction, instead of lashing back at that person, practice humility and admit that they are right. Then, take the criticism to the Lord in prayer. If there is validity to what they said, ask the Lord to help you change that area of your life. This is humility and humility is always a good thing!

- *See the good in people.*

While it is productive to identify, confront, and change things that we have been adversely affected by because of other people's choices, recognizing the good they have contributed to our lives has a way of putting everything in proper perspective. It keeps us from being self-centered and absorbed in self-pity as we confront our pasts and heal from them.

Often, even those who have hurt us have blessed our lives exponentially more than they have damaged them. Look at the good things people have done and think about their positive traits.

- *Don't insist on your own way all the time.*

Many of our problems originate when we demand that we get our own way. We don't want to compromise or give in.

In an effort to get their own way, people pout, manipulate, try to make others feel guilty, gripe, yell, nag, cry, ignore, and outright demand their own way.

This is childish behavior. It is not any more attractive on full grown adults than it is on little children in the grocery store checkout line who are throwing a temper tantrum to try to get Mom to buy them candy.

- *Control yourself.*

Some people try to control other people. Instead of trying to control other people, control yourself. If you feel the need to control, control *your* thoughts…*your* words…*your* actions…*your* attitude.

Temperance (self control) is one of the fruit of the Spirit (Galatians 5:23). Note that this fruit is not *other*-control, but *self*-control.

Proverbs 25:28 says, "He that hath no rule over his own spirit is like a city that is broken down, and without walls." In biblical times, for a city to have no walls was practically an invitation for the enemy to overthrow it. A broken down city without walls left the people vulnerable to attack.

"Rule" means to control, to take dominion, and to have authority. When we do not take control over our own spirits, words, and thoughts, we feel vulnerable and insecure.

Often, people turn their attention away from their need to control themselves and try to control others instead. This proverb says each person needs to rule his "own spirit," not everyone else's. We need to focus on the things in our own lives that need to change instead of constantly trying to control and fix others.

- *Realize that personality conflicts are normal.*

There are several different personality types. Some people are outgoing and loud; others are reticent and quiet. Some people are doers; others are thinkers. Some people are warm and open and love big groups; others prefer talking to people one-on-one.

Personality conflicts are inevitable, even in churches and families. You will not "click" with everyone in your life. But that's okay. It is normal to not "connect" with everyone but you can still be kind to them. Accept that God has blessed us with a variety of personalities to make the world an interesting place.

You might find it helpful to study the major personality types. That way, when someone grates against you and it is nothing more than a personality difference, you can prevent a conflict by not making a mountain out of a molehill.

- *View conflict in a positive light.*

Consider personality differences and conflicts as opportunities for personal character growth to develop the fruit of the Spirit in your life.

Some people bring out the best in us. It is easy to love those people. Other people bring out the worst in us. We find it a bit more challenging to love these people. They cause attitudes to surface from within us that we did not even know were there. I have been around people like this and been surprised when I responded in ways I would not normally respond. Some people are just aggravating to be around and they make it easy for us to say or do things we would not normally say or do.

We can be thankful for these people, though, because they reveal in us little nuances that we would not see otherwise. Those difficult people are actually blessings in disguise!

Differences and conflicts can be painful, but in the long run, they improve the quality of our relationships and help us grow in God.

- *Do not retaliate.*

If someone else says something wrong, don't say something wrong in return. If you do, you are adopting their problem and allowing it to poison you.

Another person's bad attitude or irrational response is not your problem. Don't make their problem yours by retaliating. I Peter 3:9 tells us to not return "evil for evil, or railing for railing."

Pray and ask the Lord to help you stay calm. Whether it is a customer, your spouse, or child, sometimes people are just blowing off steam from stress in their own lives. You can help defuse the situation by being considerate and calm.

- *Pray and read the Bible for guidance.*

In all relationships of any significant depth, there will come testing times, times of conflict of some sort or another. How these conflicts are resolved will determine the future of the relationship.

The Bible gives many instructions about conflict resolution, such as controlling anger and exercising self-control. The very fact that such information is in the Bible indicates that we will have opportunities to use it.

Pray and then wait for God to speak to you with particular Scriptures to guide you through your times of conflict resolution. He can give you specific Scriptures for your particular situation.

Put on therefore, as the elect of God, holy and beloved,
bowels of mercies, kindness, humbleness of mind,
meekness, longsuffering;
Forbearing one another, and forgiving one another,
if any man have a quarrel against any:
even as Christ forgave you, so also do ye.

And above all these things put on charity,
which is the bond of perfectness.
And let the peace of God rule in your hearts,
to the which also ye are called in one body;
and be ye thankful.

Colossians 3:12-15

CHAPTER 12

Rise Above

DOWN UNDER

The world, the devil, and our own carnal nature will try to bring us down. The enemy of our souls wants us to live the low life. The residual effects of our past might tell us that we are defeated and we will never amount to anything.

Some people cannot envision their lives as being any better than the environment in which they were raised. So they live at a much lower level of existence than God designed for them.

Often, people's conversation reflects their defeatist mentality. They talk about negative things because they can't imagine a better life for themselves.

Several phrases in the English language make room for us to express how it feels to live Down Under. "I'm feeling *under* the weather." "I guess I'm doing okay, *under* the circumstances."

Down and out. *Down* on one's luck. *Down* the drain. *Down* the tubes. *Down* in the mouth. *Down* in the dumps. *Down* for the count.

UP ABOVE

The Psalmist wrote, "The LORD is high *above* all nations, and his glory *above* the heavens" (Psalm 113:4). "For I know that the LORD is great, and that our Lord is *above* all gods" (Psalm 135:5).

God is the greatest. His glory is matchless and He is without compare. He is superior to every philosophy and ideology that man can dream up.

God is holy, meaning that He is distinct, absolutely unique, and one-of-a-kind. He has no equal. Isaiah 40:18 asks, "To whom then will ye liken God? or what likeness will ye compare unto him?"

God made Himself known to us in the man Christ Jesus. Ephesians 1:21 says that Christ is "Far *above* all principality, and power, and might, and dominion, and every name that is named, not only in this world, but also in that which is to come."

Philippians 2:9 says, "Wherefore God also hath highly exalted him, and given him a name which is *above* every name."

To the curious Jews, Jesus said, "Ye are from beneath; I am from *above*: ye are of this world; I am not of this world" (John 8:23).

Clearly, Jesus is above all powers, all human and spiritual authorities, and all names. But He is not just above. Ephesians 1:21 says that He is *far* above.

He is so far above that He is in another dimension altogether.

A HAND UP

Okay, so we understand that our God is a superlative God. What does that mean to us on a personal level? Can a God so majestic and so transcendent care about His creations – men and women, boys and girls, toddlers and senior citizens? Does He notice our pain, our hurt? Does He celebrate our happy times with us?

The beauty of the redemption plan is that God came down to our level when we could not rise to His. He is Emmanuel: God with us. He can relate to us on a human level.

This transition comes with many benefits, one of which is power to rise above things we cannot overcome on our own. When we begin to serve God, we realize that we truly can do all things through Christ who strengthens us (Philippians 4:13). Ephesians 3:20 says that God "is able to do exceeding abundantly *above* all that we ask or think, according to the power that worketh in us." If we stay yoked together with the All Mighty, His power will work in us and we can't help but be victorious.

God offers us His hand and empowers us to achieve what we could never achieve on our own. It is a hand up, a step up from the carnal realm to a life with Him that is supernatural, beautiful, and holy.

JERUSALEM WHICH IS ABOVE

"But Jerusalem which is *above* is free, which is the mother of us all" (Galatians 4:26). The writer of Galatians referred to the Church as "Jerusalem which is *above*."

The prophet Micah said that there would come a time when many nations would say "Let us go *up* to the mountain of the LORD, and to the house of the God of Jacob" (Micah 4:2). In Jerusalem was the Temple, and in the Temple was the Shekinah presence of God.

The literal city of Jerusalem is located on a mountain. It is elevated above surrounding valleys. Its high position would have made the Temple visible and noticeable.

The writer of Galatians referred to the New Testament church as "Jerusalem which is *above*." Just as the literal city of Jerusalem and its magnificent Temple were elevated, so does God elevate His Church. The Church is of Heavenly origin.

God's desire is that we learn to live *above*, in a way that causes us to rise above our circumstances and the dreariness of life, elevated and encouraged by our faith in Christ.

ABOVE AND BEYOND

In order to enjoy the superior quality of life God has for us, we must do a few simple things.

Colossians 3:1-2 tells us, "If ye then be risen with Christ, seek those things which are *above*, where

Christ sitteth on the right hand of God. Set your affection on things *above*, not on things on the earth."

If we want to enjoy Heavenly blessings, we must "seek those things which are *above*" and set our "affection on things *above*."

Our focus must not be on this earth, but on God Himself and things pertaining to His kingdom: Truth, love, and righteousness.

James 3:15 and 17 read, "This wisdom descendeth not from above, but is earthly, sensual, devilish. But the wisdom that is from *above* is first pure, then peaceable, gentle, and easy to be intreated, full of mercy and good fruits, without partiality, and without hypocrisy."

What beautiful benefits accompany "the wisdom that is from *above*." We must reject the wisdom of this world which is in direct opposition to the wisdom of God (I Corinthians 1:18-25; 3:18-19).

If we do these things – seek those things which are above, set our affection on things above, reject the wisdom of this world and embrace the wisdom from above – we will have incomparable joy and peace from above.

HIGHER GROUND

I'm pressing on the upward way,
New heights I'm gaining every day;
Still praying as I'm onward bound,
Lord, plant my feet on higher ground.

Lord, lift me up and let me stand,
By faith, on Heaven's tableland,
A higher plane than I have found;
Lord, plant my feet on higher ground.

My heart has no desire to stay
Where doubts arise and fears dismay;
Though some may dwell where those abound,
My prayer, my aim, is higher ground.

I want to live above the world,
Though Satan's darts at me are hurled;
For faith has caught the joyful sound,
The song of saints on higher ground.

I want to scale the utmost height
And catch a gleam of glory bright;
But still I'll pray till heav'n I've found,
"Lord, plant my feet on higher ground."[1]

ABOVE AND NOT BELOW

In Deuteronomy 28, God described in detail how He would bless the children of Israel if they would keep His commandments and walk in His ways. In verse 13, He promised that He would make them "the head, and not the tail; and thou shalt be *above* only, and thou shalt not be beneath." What a promise!

If we draw a spiritual analogy from this passage, if we will also walk according to God's Word, we will be on top of the world, instead of buried in its rubble. We will be "the head and not the tail." We will live above and not below.

Ephesians 3:16-21 is a fitting conclusion to this chapter and book. It is a rich passage that exalts the greatness of our God who is above all.

That he would grant you,
according to the riches of his glory,
to be strengthened with might by his Spirit in the inner man;
That Christ may dwell in your hearts by faith;
that ye, being rooted and grounded in love,
May be able to comprehend with all saints what is the breadth,
and length, and depth, and height;
And to know the love of Christ, which passeth knowledge,
that ye might be filled with all the fulness of God.
Now unto him that is able to do
exceeding abundantly above all that we ask or think,
according to the power that worketh in us,
Unto him be glory in the church by Christ Jesus throughout all ages, world without end.

Amen.

ENDNOTES

THE BUSYNESS BUSINESS

1. Linda Clare and Kristen Johnson Ingram, *Revealed* (Grand Rapids, MI: Baker Publishing Group, 2005), 107.
2. Vonda Skelton, *Seeing Through the Lies* (Ventura, CA: Regal Books, Gospel Light, 2007), 49.
3. Ibid, 55-56.
4. Patrick Morley, *The Seven Seasons of a Man's Life* (Grand Rapids, MI: Zondervan Publishing House, 1995), 268.

STUFFED

1. Daniel L. Segraves, *Ancient Wisdom for Today's World* (Hazelwood, MO: Word Aflame Press, 1990), 149 and 173.
2. Song Lyrics, "I Believe in a Hill Called Mount Calvary," Dale Oldham, Gloria Gaither, William J. Gaither, Gaither Music Company, 1968.
3. *Webster's Revised Unabridged Dictionary*, (Springfield, MA: G and C Merriam Co., 1913), 311.

PLAY THE GAME

1. Ralph Waldo Emerson
2. Song Lyrics, "Count Your Blessings," Johnson Oatman, Jr., 1897, Public Domain
3. William Arthur Ward

WORRY REMEDY
1. *Webster's Revised Unabridged Dictionary*, (Springfield, MA: G and C Merriam Co., 1913), 1666.

MY ENEMY, MY FRIEND
1. http://www.oxforddictionaries.com/us/definiton/american_english/emotion
2. http://www.psychologytoday.com/blog/the-brain-and-emotional-intelligence/201104/are-women-more-emotionally-intelligent-men

RISE ABOVE
1. Song Lyrics, "Higher Ground," Johnson Oatman, Jr., 1898, Public Domain

Other Books by Sylvia Ferrin

FOOD FOR THOUGHT
A Healthy Temple for a Holy God

COOKING WITH WISDOM
A Collection of Naturally Delicious Recipes

WALKING ANCIENT PATHS
Gleanings from the Holy Land

FINALLY FREE
Workbook and Discussion Guide

BEYOND ORDINARY
Life in the Potter's Hands

MIRROR IMAGE
Beautiful in God's Sight

MIRROR IMAGE
Workbook and Discussion Guide

To Order:
Website: www.magnifytheword.com
Online Bookstore: www.mkt.com/FerrinBookstore
Email: sylviaferrin@hotmail.com